Apostle of Liberty

George Washington is one of the most significant men in all of history. When it comes to the advancement of liberty, he may well be the *most* significant. His contemporaries acknowledged God's hand in his selection as commander of the Continental army and later as president, believing that, without him, America would not have prevailed in the Revolution or prospered as a new nation founded in liberty.

He provided the leadership to hold the troops together during the Revolutionary War, and once the war was won, he rebuffed an attempt to make him king of the United States, thereby preventing a monarchy or military rule.

Apostle of Liberty: The World-Changing Leadership of George Washington is a biography of the great man, but in truth it is more than a mere biography. It also looks at his unique qualities as a leader and how those qualities marked him as a leader among leaders. In doing so, it reveals a man whose greatness did not stem from oratorical skills, superior knowledge, or brilliant military tactics, but rather from virtue. He understood his duty and his proper role, and he pursued them with invincible resolution. Largely, this was due to his belief that God in His providence had chosen him to lead the new nation—founded on civil, religious, and economic liberty—and that the experiment that had begun under his leadership as president of the Constitutional Convention and was successful under his leadership in battle would also prosper under his leadership and change the world if given the opportunity to succeed.

Apostle
of Liberty

OTHER BOOKS IN THE LEADERS IN ACTION SERIES

Apostle of Liberty

THE WORLD-CHANGING LEADERSHIP OF GEORGE WASHINGTON

LEADERS
IN
ACTION

STEPHEN McDOWELL

DAVID VAUGHAN, GENERAL EDITOR

CUMBERLAND HOUSE
NASHVILLE, TENNESSEE

APOSTLE OF LIBERTY

PUBLISHED BY CUMBERLAND HOUSE PUBLISHING, INC.

431 Harding Industrial Drive

Nashville, Tennessee 37211

Cover design by Gore Studio, Nashville, Tennessee

Library of Congress Cataloging-in-Publication Data

McDowell, Stephen, 1954–

    Apostle of liberty : the world-changing leadership of George Washington / Stephen McDowell.

        p.   cm. — (Leaders in action)

    Includes bibliographical references and index.

    1. Washington, George, 1732–1799—Influence. 2. Washington, George, 1732–1799—Military leadership. 3. Washington, George, 1732–1799—Ethics. 4. Character—Case studies. 5. Political leadership—United States—Case studies. 6. United States—History—Revolution, 1775–1783. 7. United States—Politics and government—1775–1783. 8. United States—Politics and government—1783–1809. 9. Presidents—United States—Biography. 10. Generals—United States—Biography. I. Title. II. Series.

E312.17.M395 2007

973.4'1092—dc22   2007013030

ISBN: 978-1-68442-349-1 (hc)

ISBN: 978-1-68442-348-4 (pbk.)

For my son Philip,
who is fulfilling his duty
to God and country
through service as a captain
in the U.S. Army in Iraq

Contents

Foreword

*D*URING A recent trip to Mount Vernon, my wife and I visited the nearby gift shop. As I browsed through the many books on Washington and colonial life, I was struck by the lack of attention given to Washington's religious faith. Only a few books seemed to suggest that religion was an important part of Washington's life. Most suggested that he was either a deist or a lukewarm Anglican whose religion was primarily for public consumption.

For instance, historian Gordon Wood stated: "It is true that many of the distinguished political leaders of the Revolution were not very emotionally religious. At best, they only passively believed in organized Christianity, and at worst they scorned or ridiculed it. Most were deists or lukewarm churchgoers and scornful of religious emotion and enthusiasm. Washington, for example, was a frequent churchgoer, but he scarcely referred to God as anything but 'the Great Disposer of events,' and in all his voluminous papers he never mentioned Jesus Christ." Such is the accepted "wisdom" of the academy.

What is shocking about this statement, however, is that everything asserted here is either false or only partly true. First, Washington and the other Founders were predominantly religious men. Of the fifty-two delegates to the Constitutional Convention, twenty-eight were Episcopalians, eight were Presbyterians, and there were two each of Congregationalists, Lutherans, Dutch Reformed, Methodists, and Roman Catholics. Oh, yes, there were three deists—at best. Washington, of course, was an Episcopalian his entire life, regularly attended church, served as a vestryman (church trustee), and regularly donated generous sums to support a number of churches. While in the military, he often conducted worship services when a chaplain was not available. This is hardly a "passive" belief in organized Christianity.

Not only did Washington never scorn or ridicule Christianity, but while serving in the military, he would not permit any under his command to show the least disrespect for God or Christianity. As he said in a September 14, 1775, letter to Col. Benedict Arnold: "I also give it in Charge to you to avoid all Disrespect to or Contempt of The Religion of the Country [Canada] and its Ceremonies. Prudence, Policy, and a true Christian Spirit, will lead us to look with compassion upon their Errors [in doctrine] without insulting them. While we are contending for our own Liberty we should be very cautious of violating the Rights of Conscience in others, ever considering that God alone is the Judge of the Hearts of Men, and to him only in this Case, they are answerable."

While Washington observed his religious duties, he encouraged his troops to do likewise. Consider his general order for May 15, 1776: "The General commands all officers, and soldiers, to pay strict obedience to the Orders of the Continental Congress, and by their unfeigned, and pious observance of their religious duties, incline the Lord, and Giver of Victory, to prosper our arms."

Notice Washington's use of "Lord" and "Giver of Victory." Throughout his writings and speeches, Washington used a variety of names for God (not simply Wood's claim of "Great Disposer of Events"), including "Almighty," "Almighty God," "Father of All Mercies," "Creator," "Gracious God," "Jehovah," "Lord,"and "Wonder-working Deity." And oh, yes, he called God "Jesus Christ." In a May 22, 1779, speech to the Delaware chiefs, Washington said: "You do well to wish to learn our arts and ways of life, and above all, the religion of Jesus Christ. These will make you a greater and happier people than you are."

As for Washington's lack of religious emotion (that is, the claim that he was "lukewarm"), one does not have to be a fanatic to be sincere. In fact, not only was his denomination High Church, but Washington was also temperamentally reserved. In addition, he was a polished gentleman who believed excessive displays of emotion (about *anything,* not just religion) were an inappropriate breach of decorum. Washington actually tried to live by the "rules of civility" that he penned as a young man. Religious "emotion" (a better word is "conviction") need not be extreme to be deep and sincere. As Chief Justice John Marshall, who knew Washington, said: "Without making ostentatious professions of religion, he was a sincere believer in the Christian faith, and a truly devout man."

That a secular historian, who has no personal experience of religious faith, should presume to judge the depth of a man's religious devotion is a very telling example of humanistic hubris. Yet it only goes to show that in history, as in love, beauty is in the eye of the beholder. In other words, we often see that which is most agreeable to our own inclinations. So I suppose, given the secular bent of the modern (or should I say postmodern) intellectual class, we should not be surprised that Washington's religious faith is often downplayed or ignored.

Thankfully, however, we have Stephen McDowell's work in hand to set Washington's religious faith in the context of his multifaceted life. You will discover that from his earlier days as a surveyor, to his military career, to his attainment of the highest office in the land, Washington was guided by a profoundly religious view of life. He not only attended church, but Washington faithfully performed private devotions where he meditated on the Scriptures and prayed while on his knees (not very "lukewarm" to me). He sought God's guidance and protection, and from all the accounts of his military battles, he received it. He sought God's glory, and from his example as a gentleman, a statesman, and a Christian, he rendered it.

Contrary to the false picture of Washington that now "prevails" in the academy, through reading McDowell, you will come to know and honor the Washington that our forefathers knew and loved. And knowing him, you will have before you one of the finest examples of leadership the world has ever known—an example worthy of both your admiration and emulation. As Abigail

Adams said of him: "No man ever lived, more deservedly beloved and respected. . . . If we look through the whole tenor of his Life, History will not produce to us a Parallel."

David J. Vaughan

INTRODUCTION

*G*EORGE WASHINGTON is one of the most significant men in history. Regarding the direct advancement of civil and political liberty, he may well be the most significant champion in all history. Certainly he was the central figure in bringing a new era of liberty to the world in modern times. Abraham Lincoln observed: "Washington is the mightiest name of earth—long since mightiest in the cause of civil liberty, still mightiest in moral reformation. On that name no eulogy is expected. It cannot be. To add brightness to the sun or glory to the name of Washington is alike impossible. Let none attempt it."[1]

Founding Father Fisher Ames noted that Washington changed the standard of human greatness.[2] One biographer wrote, "Washington was without an equal, was unquestionably the greatest man that the world has produced in the last one thousand years."[3] Thomas Paine observed: "By common consent, Washington is regarded as not merely the Hero of the American Revolution, but the World's Apostle of Liberty."[4]

A figure in history like Washington did not just arise by happenstance. It was the near unanimous consent of early Americans that Washington, like Esther of old, had "come to the Kingdom for such a time as this." President Calvin Coolidge concurred in a speech to Congress on Washington's Birthday, February 22, 1927, saying there would be no America without Washington; therefore, "we can only indicate our reverence for him and thank the Divine Providence which sent him to serve and inspire his fellow men."[5]

God raised up George Washington to play a vital role in bringing liberty to mankind and advancing His kingdom in the earth. While modern historians, lacking a providential view of history, ignore such ideas, contemporaries of Washington propounded this truth. The Earl of Buchan wrote to Martha Washington upon hearing of the death of her husband: "He was one of those whom the Almighty in successive ages has chosen or raised up to promote the ultimate designs of his goodness and mercy, in the gradual melioration [improvement] of his creatures, and the coming of his kingdom which is in heaven."[6]

In 1932, commemorative events occurred in more than 275 cities in 81 countries honoring Washington on the two-hundredth anniversary of his birth, including speeches, sermons, plays, ceremonies, statues, renamed streets and bridges, tree plantings, and newspaper articles and editorials. Rulers, parliaments, statesmen, and leaders in education, religion, business, and culture took part in this unprecedented series of observances. Americans had celebrated Washington's birthday ever since he led the nation to victory in the Revolutionary War. The world now celebrated his life, because all had come to recognize his role in the advancement of liberty around the world. Sol Bloom, the director of the George Washington Bicentennial Commission, noted that the addresses of statesmen and historians in other nations gave accounts of Washington's worldwide influence: "The greatness of George Washington as it now shines upon mankind, finds reflection in the liberty and political enlightenment that encircle the earth."[7]

At one commemorative event, the Reverend Hugh Grant delivered a sermon summarizing how Washington "brought liberty, not only to his own people, but advanced it to the peoples of the world." He noted, "In God's Providence George Washington was chosen to take one step forward in the free determination of a people. A movement that today has conquered the earth." Grant concluded, "God was behind the movement of liberty" in America, and Washington was at its head; God was at work "to write a new page in the advancement of liberty to the world."[8]

God is still behind the movement of liberty in the world today, for He is the author of liberty. This crucial message is clearly revealed in the life, character, and words of "the World's Apostle of Liberty."

Washington's own writings comprise scores of volumes, and they are still being compiled. The intent of this book is not to add new facts about his life but to present his life from a perspective that most historians ignore; that is, a providential perspective, which was the view Washington held of events in history. The second part of this book highlights the qualities of character in Washington's life that were essential to his role as the

"Father of his Country." His life and character offer an example today of what is necessary to preserve the great liberty Americans possess. We have this liberty, in large part, thanks to Washington's life work.

Washington acknowledged the providence of God throughout his life, and he regularly sought His guidance. In reviewing the events of the previous two years of the Revolution, he wrote in 1778, "The hand of Providence has been so conspicuous in all of this, that he must be worse than an infidel that lacks faith, and more than wicked, that has not gratitude enough to acknowledge his obligations."[9] Washington would view many of today's writers as worse than infidels and more than wicked because they fail to acknowledge God's hand in history or in the life of Washington. Some may say I have emphasized Providence too much in this book, but this would not be the view of Washington, for throughout I quote him in acknowledging God's providence in the various stages of his life.

Washington believed that morality and faith in God are essential for liberty and happiness in a nation. His life, in word and action, demonstrates to Americans today these essential pillars of society.

Washington's excellent character was acknowledged by people from all segments of society throughout America and the world, by family members and intimate friends, by those who served under him in the army and the government, by political friends and those with opposite views. Thomas Jefferson served in Washington's cabinet but held many contrary political views. He, though, testified of Washington's exemplary character:

His integrity was most pure, his justice the most inflexible I
have ever known; no motives of interest or consanguinity,
of friendship or hatred, being able to bias his decision. He
was, indeed, in every sense of the words, a wise, a good,
and a great man. . . . On the whole, his character was, in
its mass, perfect, in nothing bad, in few points indifferent;
and it may truly be said that never did nature and fortune
combine more perfectly to make a man great, and to place
him in the same constellations with whatever worthies
have merited from man an everlasting remembrance.[10]

People's high esteem for Washington grew the more
they read and heard about him. This only increased for
those who met him. Personal secretary Tobias Lear, after
living in Washington's home for two years, observed: "I
have never found a single thing that could lessen my respect for him. A complete knowledge of his honesty, uprightness, and candor in all his private transactions, has
sometimes led me to think him more than a man."[11]

Washington's character reflects his parents' training as
well as his biblical education and the influence of his
church. That character is apparent in all the occupations
of his life, in both public service and private concerns.
From early on, Washington the farmer strove to produce
the best crops possible. His reputation for quality goods
was such that any barrel stamped "George Washington,
Mount Vernon" was exempted from regular inspection in
the West Indies.[12] The qualities of the private man were
completely compatible with that of the public man.

Washington was a gift of God to the American republic
because he served as an example to the nation of the

American character. He was a pattern for this character and an example to the generations that followed. The dependence upon God, self-government, courage, industry, enterprise, public spirit, economy, and humility that Washington displayed are components of the true American character. The decline of these traits within our population today coincides with the decline in teaching about Washington in our schools. Few people today really know much about the Father of the Country. He is no longer used as an example to emulate; if anything, he is perceived as a mere relic preserved on the dollar bill. Yet the qualities he embodied are essential for the preservation of the American republic.

Washington was so esteemed by his fellow citizens that they celebrated his birthday even while he was alive. This observance continued for nearly two hundred years. Washington's birthday, however, is no longer uniquely celebrated by the nation—it has been instead morphed into the generic "Presidents' Day." This change followed the change in how history is taught in our schools, from centering on individual men and events, under the providence of God, to focusing on the generic influence of social and environmental factors and random chance. Americans must come to reacquaint themselves with the man Washington, and they must relearn his worldview and emulate his character.

ACKNOWLEDGMENTS

I HAVE GREATLY ENJOYED reading, researching, and writing about George Washington. This great man has been my hero for many years. The more I have learned about him, the more my admiration has grown for him. I would agree with Washington's personal secretary, Tobias Lear, who lived in Washington's home for two years: "I have never found a single thing that could lessen my respect for him. A complete knowledge of his honesty, uprightness, and candor in all his private transactions, has sometimes led me to think him more than a man."

He was, of course, just a man, but one whose character and contribution to history elevate him to the best of men. He is one that all other men ought to get to know. I wish I could spend many more years getting to know Washington and laboring so as to be more effective in communicating to others his character and contribution to God's work in history. Washington's life is so rich and there is so much to learn from him that years are needed to learn the many lessons he has to teach us. In this brief work, I had to omit much about his life, and I did not even begin to examine the significance of the ideas he expounded in his public writings.

I would like to thank Candy Bruner McDowell, my daughter-in-law, and Andrew McDowell, my son, for their help in researching this project. Candy moved from the West Coast in 2004 to intern with me at the Providence Foundation. During that time, she not only assisted me by compiling Washington's character qualities but also became a godly spouse for my son.

I also want to thank my wife Beth, my son John, and my daughter Caroline for being patient with me during the many nights I spent writing. Beth also reviewed and edited the text. Thanks as well to Michelle Atchley, my administrative assistant at the Providence Foundation, for her editorial feedback.

Many thanks to my friend David Barton for letting me use numerous copies of first editions of orations and sermons commemorating Washington's death and birthday, plus copies of some hard-to-find out-of-print books.

Finally, David Vaughan's editorial comments contributed greatly to this book.

CHRONOLOGY OF THE LIFE OF GEORGE WASHINGTON

1732	February 22: George is born to Augustine and Mary Washington at Wakefield, Virginia. George is baptized on April 5.
1735	Washington family moves to upper Potomac lands (later named Mount Vernon by George's half brother Lawrence).
1738	Family moves to Ferry Farm near Fredericksburg, Virginia.
1743	April 12: George's father dies at Ferry Farm. For the next few years, George lives at both Ferry Farm and with his half brother Augustine at Wakefield.
1746	George obeys his mother's wishes and does not go to sea.
1747	George begins to survey for Lord Fairfax in the Shenandoah Valley.
1748	George goes to Mount Vernon to live with Lawrence. In March, George begins a journal of his travels as he surveys in the Shenandoah Valley.
1751	Lawrence and George travel to Barbados. George contracts smallpox.
1752	July 26: Lawrence dies at Mount Vernon. George later inherits Mount Vernon when Lawrence's daughter dies and his widow remarries.
1753	George is commissioned by the governor of Virginia to deliver a message to the French to leave the Ohio Territory

that belonged to the British. His journal was published early the following year in Virginia, England, and France and began to make Washington known to many.

1754   Washington leads a force at Fort Necessity and is defeated by the French.

1755   George is providentially protected during the battle of the Monongahela where British Gen. Edward Braddock is defeated.

1756   Washington travels to New England to meet with the British commander.

1758   Washington is first elected to the Virginia House of Burgesses. He continued as a member of the Virginia legislature until the American Revolution.

1759   January 6: Washington marries Martha Dandridge Custis, a widow with two children. With marriage, he receives one-third of her large estate. He was also given charge of her two children and the management of their estates.

1763   Washington becomes a vestryman for Truro Parish.

1765   Elected as member of House of Burgesses from newly formed Fairfax County. At the meeting of the legislature, he heard Henry give his "if this be treason" speech and the Stamp Act was discussed.

1770   Washington travels to the Ohio Territory, where an Indian chief prophesies to him.

1772   First portrait of Washington is painted by Charles Wilson Peale at Mount Vernon.

1773   Martha's daughter, seventeen-year-old Martha Parke Custis, dies at Mount Vernon.

1774   Washington attends the First Continental Congress in Philadelphia.

1775   Washington attends the Second Continental Congress and in June is elected as the commander of the Continental army. He travels to Boston to assume command.

1776   Declaration of Independence is signed. Miraculous retreat from Long Island. Washington suffers defeats but obtains important victory at Trenton in December.

1777   Year begins with victory at Princeton then defeats at Brandywine and Germantown. British Gen. John Burgoyne surrenders at Saratoga. Winter quarters at Valley Forge.

1778   Battle of Monmouth.

1780   Providential discovery of Benedict Arnold's treason.

1781   Victory at Yorktown is final major battle of the war. Martha's son, John Parke Custis, dies; George adopts his two younger children.

1782   Washington rejects offer from some officers to become king.

1783   Washington thwarts military coup, writes "Circular to the Governors of the States." Peace treaty signed with Britain. In December, Washington resigns his commission as commander and returns to Mount Vernon.

1785   Jean-Antoine Houdon arrives at Mount Vernon from Paris to prepare for the statue of Washington provided for by an act of the Virginia legislature.

1787   Washington attends the Constitutional Convention in Philadelphia and is elected to preside over the proceedings. A new constitution is approved by delegates in September and sent to the states for ratification.

1789   New government goes into effect. Washington is unanimously elected as the first president under the Constitution. In April, he takes the oath of office on a Bible in New York City.

1790   Washington and the national government move to Phila-
        delphia.

1793   Washington lays the cornerstone for the Capitol in the
        new capital city, the District of Columbia. Washington is
        unanimously reelected to a second term as president.

1796   Washington delivers his Farewell Address.

1797   In March, Washington retires to Mount Vernon when his
        term expires as president.

1798   Washington commissioned as commanding general of the
        provisional army, though he never has to take the field.

1799   December 14: George Washington dies at Mount Vernon
        after a brief sickness.

Apostle
of Liberty

Part 1

The Life of George Washington

*Washington was the directing spirit without which
there would have been no independence, no
Union, no Constitution and no Republic. His ways
were the ways of truth. His influence grows. In
wisdom of action, in purity of character he stands
alone. We cannot yet estimate him. We can only
indicate our reverence for him and thank the
Divine Providence which sent him to serve and
inspire his fellow men.*

—Calvin Coolidge

*He was one of those whom the Almighty in
successive ages has chosen or raised up to
promote the ultimate designs of his goodness and
mercy, in the gradual melioration of his creatures,
and the coming of his kingdom which is in heaven.*

—The Earl of Buchan

ANCESTRY AND BIRTH

*G*EORGE WASHINGTON WAS DESCENDED from noble stock who were greatly respected and showed a spirit of independence and patriotism. Though Washington's ancestors can be traced to prominent families in sixteenth- and seventeenth-century England, he cared little about his pedigree. Responding to a gentleman who had traced his lineage, Washington wrote: "This is a subject to which I confess I have paid but very little attention. My time has been so much occupied in the busy and active scenes of life from an early period of it, that but a small portion could have been devoted to researches of this nature, even if my inclination or particular circumstances should have prompted to the inquiry."[1]

Washington's ancestors first came to America in 1657, when his great-great-grandfather John Washington settled at Pope's Head Creek in Westmoreland County, Virginia.

He was well respected by those in the area, who even named the parish after him. The family was still living there seventy-five years later when, on February 22, 1732, George was born to Augustine and Mary Washington.[2]

Not much is known of Augustine, the grandson of the original settler, "except that he was a handsome, stout, strong man, prosperous and happy, and much respected by his neighbors."[3] He was certainly a man of virtue, as he laid this foundation in the life of his famous son through example and the many life lessons he taught George.

Mary was Augustine's second wife. Before Augustine's first wife died, they had three boys and one girl, with two boys surviving to adulthood, therefore George did not have the advantage of being the oldest son. So when he was born in the four-room house at Wakefield near Pope's Creek, there was no indication he would become the founder of a new republic and one of the great men of history. It was truly the hand of Providence that prepared him, not the advantages of the world.

George Washington's main advantage was his godly upbringing. Though he did inherit a considerable amount of land, to which he added with his income as a surveyor, it was his hard work, business acumen, and frugality that caused his farms to prosper. It was this income from his farms that primarily supported him during his many years of service to his country, since for much of that time he received no salary for those services.

According to the family Bible, George was baptized on April 5 by the Reverend Roderick McCullough at the family home.[4] From birth until death, church and its activities were a regular and vital part of his life. When George was three years old, his family moved many miles up the Potomac River to Little Hunting Creek. Eight years later, George's half brother Lawrence would inherit this estate and rename it Mount Vernon. After three years here, the family moved to Ferry Farm near Fredericksburg, Virginia. Augustine and Mary had six children—George, Betty, Samuel, John Augustine, Charles, and Mildred (who died at age one)—and so George had plenty of company as he grew up.

Upbringing and Education

WASHINGTON'S PARENTS WERE HIS primary in-
structors through example, daily direction,
and formal teaching. He was raised in a plain and simple
home, experiencing the rigors of a rural life through farmwork and hunting. Not only were his physical strengths
and skills developed in this environment, but also his industry, frugality, and enjoyment of simple pleasures.

There are many anecdotal stories from George's
boyhood—the best known is the chopping down of the
cherry tree—of how his parents taught him character
qualities that formed the foundation necessary for his life
accomplishments. While many of these cannot be confirmed as actually occurring, the evidence of various character traits presented in these incidents can be seen
throughout his life. Many of these stories were printed in
various textbooks, for example, *McGuffey's Readers,* and

served as examples to generations of American youth of the importance of godly character.

From all indications, George had a happy boyhood, growing in knowledge, character, spiritual understanding, and physical skills, all of which were essential for accomplishing the mission that lay ahead of him. His parents deserve primary credit for this.

There is no record of any teachers whom George may have had or any schools he may have attended. Early on, he may have been tutored by a teacher-clergyman, and while living at Ferry Farm, he may have attended a school in Fredericksburg conducted by the Reverend James Marye. Between the ages of seven and eleven, he no doubt received the best education possible for one living in Fredericksburg.[5] If he attended a field school, it would have had the Bible as its central text, which was typical of rural schools.[6] His formal schooling, if any, was only for a short time, and Washington never attended college. His education was centered in the home.

His mother read to him the best books she could find and directed him in other studies. In addition to the Bible, one book she read daily, which had a great influence in his life, was Matthew Hale's *Contemplations, Moral and Divine.*[7] The thoroughly biblical ideas and principles taught by Hale can be seen in many of Washington's later writings. One chapter on "The Great Audit" gives a report of a good steward to his master in which he says, "I have therefore always taken this care, not to set my heart upon my reputation . . . ; and if . . . my reputation be soiled by evil or man, I will patiently bear it, and content myself with the serenity of my own conscience."[8] His words and action when some people tried to displace him as the commanding general during the Revolutionary War well express these sentiments of Matthew Hale.[9]

George's home-centered education produced a man who had all the understanding necessary to support liberty; he had a liberal arts education. Though not of the brilliance of a Thomas Jefferson or a John Quincy Adams, Washington had the strength of sound reasoning so necessary for the important decisions he faced throughout his life. While his literary style was not that of a Shakespeare or other such genius, the force of his ideas and the sheer volume of writings, more than forty volumes to date, had a great impact on advancing liberty and political happiness.

His father, a planter, acquired large landholdings, some through inheritance, but much through his own industry and business skills. These skills were passed on to George. Augustine died when George was eleven years old, but George carried the early training of his father with him throughout his life. He was very industrious in his studies, as in everything he did.

His mother continued to educate him, though George was possibly sent to a school conducted by Henry Williams while living with his half brother Augustine at Wakefield. Grammar and mathematics were Williams's forte, but he "knew as little of Latin as Balaam's ass!"[10] George continued to develop his ability to communicate his ideas in a strong, straightforward manner, which also marked his public and private writings throughout his life.

From a young age, George stood out as a leader with a firm sense of justice, whether it was commanding the boys as they played or when his playmates chose him as their umpire in quarrels. They would say, "Ask George Washington and whatever he says is right, we'll agree to."[11] He was known as a peacemaker.

George's interest in military affairs came from the example of his half brother Lawrence, who served in the British navy. He saw Lawrence dressed in his uniform and heard him speak of military scenes. Lawrence's friends would also visit Mount Vernon, where George would listen to them talk during dinner. (George lived with Lawrence during some of his youthful years after his father's death.) George also was known to form his young friends into companies and run them through drills and command them in mock battles. He always took the lead and naturally applied his developing character qualities of order, promptness, and thoroughness. His fiery passion also showed itself during these games, yet he was marked with a self-control that would be of great importance in later events.

George kept a notebook of his exercises in arithmetic and geometry while attending Williams's school. He also kept notebooks of his other studies, one containing a whole course of bookkeeping and business forms (thus planting seeds for his business skills) and one with poetry. Of greater importance was his notebook in which he copied "Rules of Civility & Decent Behaviour in Company and Conversation" comprised of 110 rules that taught important character traits, good behavior qualities, and ideas of compassion, respect, modesty, and cleanliness. These rules included such things as: think before you speak, do not hum or drum your fingers in company of others, honor your parents, and speak of God with reverence.[12]

The use of notebooks in Washington's education helped to develop his character as well as reveal his character. Historian Jared Sparks observed that Washington's copybooks "are remarkable for the care with which they were kept, the neatness and uniformity of the handwriting, the beauty of the diagrams, and a precise method and arrangement in copying out tables and columns of figures."[13] This order and preciseness are displayed throughout his life in his writings, dress, farm management style, governance of the army, and scheduling as president.

His later journals, ledgers, and surveying details grew out of these early notebooks. Keeping notebooks helped to fix the ideas in his mind as well as develop habits of orderliness, neatness, and attention to detail. In addition, the practice of writing down so many things laid the foundation for the voluminous number of letters he would write throughout his lifetime, around forty thousand. He was one of the most prolific writers of the Founding Fathers.

Washington displayed excellent penmanship throughout his life. He kept detailed business records, and he made minutes of everything connected with his duties. Without his great writing abilities, developed early by the notebook method of education, Washington would never have been able to accomplish all that he did. Washington Irving commented, "To the achievements of his indefatigable pen we may trace the most fortunate turns in the current of our Revolutionary affairs."[14] It could almost be said that writing letters was his life's work.

Physical Skills and Moral Development

*W*ASHINGTON INHERITED A LARGE-FRAMED, tall, strong body. Rigorous exercise in his youth helped to develop his powerful physique and athletic skills. He delighted in outdoor activities—running, leaping, pitching, and wrestling. No one could match him in horsemanship, running a race, wrestling, or pitching. One gentleman said, "Egad! He ran wonderfully! We had nobody hereabouts that could come near him."[15] His kinsman and playmate Lewis Willis had "often seen him throw a stone across the Rappahannock, at the lower ferry of Fredericksburg," a grand feat that few could perform as the distance was not small. This is probably where the story originated of his throwing a dollar across the river, but as a frugal, responsible boy, he certainly would not have wasted a dollar in this pursuit. No doubt, Washington had a strong arm; he once threw a rock to the top of Natural Bridge, a height of 215 feet.[16] His strength and athletic skills stayed with him throughout his life.

His frame was powerful, but he also carried himself with grace and style. His appearance and stately demeanor made a great impression upon all who met him. He grew to a height of about six feet two inches and was a head taller than the average man (about five feet six inches tall). His height and frame produced an imposing figure. In addition, his athleticism and dignity made his appearance grand.

Washington loved horses and was called "the best rider in Virginia."[17] He developed this skill from a young age, which proved providential as he spent about half his life on horseback. He always kept good horses and took excellent care of them.

Many great men have described the central role their mothers played in their success. This was true of George Washington, who attributed the training of his mother as "the foundation of his fortune and his fame."[18] Throughout his life, Washington was reserved in his manners yet sociable. He was serious in his conversation but enjoyed conversing. His presence produced awe, but in a kindly way. The influence of his mother is evident, as she imparted to George much of his deportment and manner. Childhood friend and cousin Lawrence Washington described the home of George's mother:

> I was often there with George, his playmate, schoolmate, and young man's companion. Of the mother I was ten times more afraid than I ever was of my own parents. She

awed me in the midst of her kindness, for she was, indeed, truly kind. I have often been present with her sons, proper tall fellows too, and we were all as mute as mice; and even now, when time has whitened my locks, and I am the grand-parent of a second generation, I could not behold that remarkable woman without feelings it is impossible to describe. Whoever has seen that awe-inspiring air and manner so characteristic in the Father of his Country, will remember the matron as she appeared when the presiding genius of her well-ordered household, commanding and being obeyed.[19]

Mary Washington was also a very competent manager. After her husband died, she capably directed the affairs of her family and farm, seeing that they were productive. Even in her old age she vowed, "I can manage my affairs myself."[20] When George offered for her to live in his home, she responded, "I thank you, George, but I prefer being independent."[21]

George's half brothers, especially Lawrence, contributed greatly to his education. Lawrence, who was fourteen years older than George, became a close friend and surrogate father to him. Lord Fairfax, a neighbor to Lawrence, also gave much input into George's life. While George lived at Mount Vernon with Lawrence, he often visited the Fairfax home at Belvoir, and thus was introduced to the highest plantation class in America. Taken as a whole, all his early training and mentoring had the greatest positive effect. That there were no negative influences operating upon George in his early life is one great reason for his overall excellent character.

George loved outdoor activities throughout his life, from exploring the woods, to surveying the wilderness, to hunting fox, to riding on his farms. His spirit of self-denial enabled him to perform his duties and spend long hours in correspondence, councils, and offices, while he would much rather be in the open air on a horse.

God not only prepared George through the training of his parents but also used his experiences in life to assure that he was well equipped to fulfill his destiny. All these things helped instill in him those character qualities essential to fulfilling his calling.

When Augustine Washington died suddenly on April 12, 1743, Lawrence inherited the farm in Fairfax County that he named Mount Vernon in honor of the British admiral under whom he had served in the navy. George's share of the inheritance was Ferry Farm, but his mother was left in charge of the property of the underage children. Under her care, the farm prospered and the children grew up to be respectable and productive.

Augustine's other son, also named Augustine, inherited the old home at Bridge's Creek, called Wakefield. As mentioned above, George lived here for a period after his father's death and may have attended school for a short time. Unlike his older half brothers, he was not sent to school in England. George received the education necessary to be an honest and successful planter. His mother believed plantation life would produce great satisfaction and joy for George.

George often visited Lawrence while he was alternately living at Bridge's Creek and Ferry Farm. It was during these visits that he first met William Fairfax, whose daughter Lawrence had married, and Thomas Fairfax, a cousin of William. Thomas owned an immense tract of land in western Virginia. These acquaintances proved to be of great importance to Washington in his career as a surveyor, in his growth as a man of principle and knowledge, and in his introduction to the highest society. It was probably through these friends that Lawrence procured a warrant for midshipman for George when he was but fourteen years of age. George was prepared to become a navy man, but his mother objected, and he acquiesced to her wishes (see pages 188–90, "Obedience").

During his visits to Mount Vernon, George particularly benefited by receiving military training. George Muse, an adjutant who had served with Lawrence, loaned him books on tactics and shared with him much from his own experience. George also learned to fence from Jacob Van Braam. These experiences were an important part of his preparation for his future military career.[22]

THE SURVEYOR

*W*ASHINGTON DEVELOPED SURVEYING SKILLS early on. He had an aptitude for geometry and trigonometry and saw surveying as a useful profession. As early as August 1745, George began making notes on surveying in his notebooks. His first practical training possibly came from James Genn, an experienced surveyor.[23] His habits of neatness and accuracy were reinforced in surveying. This skill would later be of great advantage to him when he purchased new properties and developed his lands.

In March 1748, sixteen-year-old George traveled to the western wilderness of Virginia with William Fairfax, chief surveyor James Genn, and a small group of men to explore and survey the immense tracts of wild land for Lord Thomas Fairfax. While here, he not only acquired important surveying experience, but he also gained a personal knowledge of the country and a spirit of self-reliance, which aided him in his later duties as a commander. During this trip, the party encountered many difficulties, dangers, and challenges. The weather was often bad; they mostly slept on the ground, in the rain at times. They worked hard and swam their horses across many streams. Provisions were poor. George kept a diary of his trip with accounts of the surveying activities, but he kept a separate journal of incidents during the trip and various notes.[24] His "journey over the mountains" began on March 11, 1748, and concluded on April 13, 1748, when he arrived back at Mount Vernon.

In his journals, he describes meeting "thirty odd Indians coming from War with only one Scalp" and witnessing an Indian "War Daunce" on March 23:

> There Manner of Dauncing is as follows Viz. They clear a Large Circle & make a great Fire in the Middle then seats themselves around it the Speaker makes a grand Speech telling them in what Manner they are to Daunce after he has finish'd the best Dauncer Jumps up as one awaked out of a Sleep & Runs & Jumps about the Ring in a most comicle Manner he is followd by the Rest then begins there Musicians to Play the Musick is a Pot half of Water with a Deerskin Streched over it as tight as it can & a goard with some Shott in it to Rattle & a Piece of an horses Tail tied to it to make it look fine the one keeps Rattling and the other Drumming all the While the others is Dauncing.[25]

On April 2, he recorded: "Last Night was a blowing & Rainy night. Our Straw catch'd a Fire that we were laying upon & was luckily Preserv'd by one of our Mens awaking when it was in a [flame]."[26] This is one of many times in his life when George was providentially saved from harm.

During the trip, he rarely slept in a house, and even then, he would have to sleep on the floor before the hearth. He wrote, "I have never had my clothes off, but have lain and slept in them, except the few nights we slept at Fredericksburg." His good reward of a doubloon every day is what made these days "pass off tolerably."[27] The satisfaction of Lord Fairfax in Washington's work was also a cherished reward.

George continued to visit and be influenced by the Fairfaxes. They introduced him to the formal manners of a gentleman, and they contributed to his growth as a man—a man who would ultimately bring much change to the Fairfaxes. Mason Weems noted: "Little did the old gentleman expect that he was educating a youth, who should one day dismember the British empire, and break his own heart."[28]

He kept up surveying work for about three years. Through this work he was introduced to many men of influence and wealth. Much of his surveying was in the west. The time he spent in the wilderness was a providential preparation for his later work in the army during the French and Indian War and as commander during the Revolution. He also used his income to buy about a thousand acres of land.

In 1751, Washington fulfilled a family duty by accompanying his brother Lawrence to the West Indies in hopes of seeing a worsening lung ailment subside in a healing environment. They arrived in Barbados in early Novem-

ber after a five-week voyage. As he had done before,
George kept a diary, but it is largely a matter-of-fact re-
counting of daily events, though often containing the
minutia of his activities. However, his modesty in men-
tioning personal difficulties is apparent in that, shortly
after his arrival, he contracted smallpox (on November
16) and was extremely ill for three weeks, but he barely
mentions this in his diary.[29] Biographer Edward Everett
wrote that his contracting smallpox at this time and place
"was one of the providential events of his life."[30] His having smallpox proved beneficial for his future in that he became immune to the disease that afflicted many in the
Revolutionary War. Smallpox swept through the army at
the siege of Boston just after Washington assumed command, and many more died from smallpox during the war
than in battle.

Washington delighted in much of his surroundings in
Barbados. He liked pineapples and other tropical fruits,
and he attended the theater, which he enjoyed throughout his life. He records that one evening he and
Lawrence rode out and "were perfectly enraptured with
the beautiful prospects which every side presented to
our view."[31]

But the climate had little effect on Lawrence's health,
and the weather was very hot with no "bodily diver-
sions,"[32] so the brothers decided to leave. George left in
December for Virginia, while Lawrence traveled to
Bermuda to see if the climate there proved better. After a
few months, his health continued to deteriorate, thus
Lawrence returned to Mount Vernon, where he died on
July 26, 1752, at the age of thirty-four. To George, this

was like losing a second father, as Lawrence had filled that role since the death of Augustine nine years before.

Lawrence left the care of his estate and family in George's hands. The events of his life were causing him to mature at an early age. Lawrence's widow would later remarry, and his daughter would die, after which George inherited Mount Vernon in accordance with Lawrence's will. George took up residence there and began a series of improvements that continued the rest of his life.[33]

THE FRENCH AND INDIAN WAR

*A*ROUND THIS TIME, George Washington was appointed by Gov. Robert Dinwiddie to be one of four adjutants general for the state of Virginia. He took the oath of office in February 1753. Given the rank of major, Washington was charged with protecting parts of the frontier that were beginning to have problems with some Indian tribes as well as French encroachment. He was to assemble and train a militia, giving the militiamen proper arms and maintaining military discipline should they be needed to defend the settlers on the frontier. Here is another important step in Washington's preparation as a military leader. His duties were initially light, and this gave him time to continue to survey the area.

In the fall of 1753, Washington volunteered for a dangerous and difficult mission: to deliver a dispatch from Governor Dinwiddie to the French on the Ohio River, instructing them to cease building forts on British land. Disputes between the English and French over this territory had been going on for years, but a recent decision by the French to erect a line of forts along the Ohio River precipitated action by the Virginia governor.

Washington left Williamsburg on October 31, commencing the 550-mile journey. After obtaining supplies and enlisting others, he headed a party of eight through the wilderness, over mountains, and through "excessive rains, Snows, & bad traveling, through many Mires & Swamps."[34] After "a continued series of bad weather,"[35] they reached the fort, where Washington delivered Dinwiddie's letter to the French commander on December 12.

After receiving the French reply, Washington headed back on what was "a tedious and very fatiguing passage."[36] The horses became nearly useless as the cold and snow increased, so Washington, anxious to make his report as soon as possible, set out on foot accompanied only by Christopher Gist. Toward the end of December, they encountered a party of Indians in league with the French. "One of them fired at Mr. Gist or me, not 15 steps, but fortunately missed."[37] This would not be the last time Washington was fired on in his lifetime with the miraculous outcome of never receiving a scratch. Gist wanted to kill the Indian, but Washington would not allow it, so they let him go on his way. Washington and Gist traveled throughout the night, in case the Indian decided to put others on their trail.[38]

The next evening, the two men reached the river, which they thought would be frozen, allowing them to walk across. Finding it flowing freely in the middle, with the edges frozen out fifty yards from the shore, they built a crude raft to cross. After a day's work with one hatchet, they launched the raft. Washington described this crossing, which could easily have ended in his death:

> Before we got half over, we were jamed in the Ice in such a Manner, that we expected every Moment our Raft wou'd sink, & we Perish; I put out my seting Pole, to try to stop the Raft, that the Ice might pass by, when the Rapidity of the Stream through it with so much Violence against the Pole, that it Jirk'd me into 10 Feet Water, but I fortunately saved my Self by catching hold of one of the Raft Logs. Notwithstanding all our Efforts we cou'd not get the Raft to either Shoar, but were oblig'd, as we were pretty near an Island, to quit our Raft & wade to it. The Cold was so extream severe, that Mr. Gist got all his Fingers, & some of his Toes Froze, & the Water was shut up so hard, that We found no Difficulty in getting off the Island on the Ice in the Morning.[39]

The matter-of-fact accounting of such extreme hardships and dangers is rather revealing of Washington's character; it also shows God's hand of preparation. Washington wrote that this eleven-week trip was "as fatiguing a journey as it is possible to conceive."[40] The trials of his troops in the Revolution during the winter at Valley Forge would prove to be even more severe.

Washington arrived in Williamsburg on January 16, 1754, and made his report to the governor. The French commander had replied that disputes over land treaties were outside his jurisdiction and should be taken up with the governor-general of Canada. He was under orders from that authority and could not leave his post. With this answer in hand, Dinwiddie issued orders to raise troops for the defense of the western lands. Washington was appointed as one of the commanders of a force that was to travel to the fork of the Ohio River and erect a fort for defensive measures. If they encountered resistance, they could use whatever force necessary "to make Prisoners of or kill and destroy them."[41]

To build support for this campaign, Dinwiddie ordered the printing of Washington's journal to the Ohio. Washington opposed the idea, but if it were to be printed, he wanted to at least rewrite his hastily composed personal journal, correcting the many errors in spelling and grammar. The governor insisted there was not time for this, thus the journal was quickly printed in Williamsburg. Copies were widely distributed and discussed in the colonies and in England, after being printed there. The courageous young George Washington became known by many.

Washington was pleased with his commission, because he wanted to advance his military career, but due to his youth and inexperience, he had no expectation of being placed in charge of the expedition. He was second in command to Joshua Fry, who had more experience in such endeavors. Fry, however, died on May 31, and Washington assumed command. To accomplish his assignment, he was promoted to lieutenant colonel, but he was not given adequate funds for the expedition. His experience in raising and equipping troops without money, as well as dealing with poorly equipped men, began here. Many of his men were without shoes and socks, and some had no shirts or coats.[42] Washington said it was "a fatiguing time to me, in managing a number of self-willed, ungovernable people."[43]

THE JUMONVILLE AFFAIR

*L*t. Col. George Washington overcame many obstacles, raised a small force, and pushed into the wilderness, discovering that the French (with an army of reportedly one thousand men) had taken over the American fort under construction at the fork of the Ohio, where the Monongahela and Allegheny rivers converge (the present-day site of Pittsburgh). Capt. Claude Pierre Pécaudy Contrecoeur and his men completed the works, naming it Fort Duquesne. This was the first open hostility in what became known in Europe as the Seven Years War and in America as the French and Indian War.

Though outnumbered, Washington pushed ahead to a place known as the Great Meadows, where the army pre-pared for a potential encounter by quickly constructing a rough fort, which Washington dubbed Fort Necessity. As it neared completion, he was informed that some French scouts and a small party had been spotted within five miles of his fort. Washington led forty men and a number of Indians out to investigate, and they came upon the French lodgment commanded by Joseph Coulon de Jumonville. Upon seeing the Virginia forces, the French grabbed their weapons, and fighting ensued for about fifteen minutes. Washington reported, "We killed 10, wounded one, and took 21 prisoners," while he lost one killed and two or three wounded.[44] Jumonville was one of those killed. The French claimed that the group was on a diplomatic mission, but their actions showed otherwise, and Washington pointed this out in a letter to Dinwiddie.[45]

Regarding this skirmish, Washington wrote his brother John Augustine, "I heard the bullets whistle, and, believe me, there is something charming in the sound."[46] On hearing this, George II said: "He would not say so, if he had been used to hear many."[47] Asked of this later, during the Revolution and after having gained such experience, Washington responded, "If I said so, it was when I was young."[48]

A few days later, a large French force attacked Washington at Fort Necessity. Greatly outnumbered and hindered by a violent storm that dampened much of the Virginians' gunpowder, and after hours of resistance, Washington's only choice was to surrender or be destroyed. The modest terms of the capitulation—the men were allowed to march off with their arms and whatever supplies they could carry—reinforced Washington's view that this was not a complete defeat but a standoff. The articles of capitulation, however, included a statement that Jumonville had been assassinated while on a diplomatic mission. A poor translation did not make this clear, and

Washington did not know he was seemingly agreeing to a French interpretation of the incident that would be used as an argument supporting the war against Britain. Washington always maintained that Jumonville headed a hostile party; he would never have signed a document stating otherwise. The Virginia governor and legislature supported his view.[49] Washington's defeated army marched out of Fort Necessity on July 4.

The French victory at Great Meadows gave them confidence to continue building the line of forts from Lake Erie, down the Ohio and Mississippi rivers, to New Orleans. Dinwiddie pressed Washington to raise a larger force to deter the French. But Washington demurred, pointing out that he lacked funds and sufficient supplies for such a campaign and adding that the coming winter season was not the time to launch such an offensive. Furthermore, his recruits were not trained for this type of operation. He wrote, "The chief part are almost naked, and scarcely a man has either shoes, stockings, or a hat. . . . There is not a man that has a blanket to secure him from cold or wet."[50] More than twenty years later he would write of similar needs to Congress during the winter at Valley Forge.

The next year, Gen. Edward Braddock arrived in Virginia with a large force and orders to defeat the French. Just prior to his appearance, a restructuring of colonial military commissions led to demotions for Washington and other Virginia officers. In response to this injustice, Washington resigned, refusing to serve at a lesser rank in Braddock's army. Braddock, however, recognized how valuable Washington would be to him, and so he asked

Washington to be his aide-de-camp. Still ambitious and desiring to learn all he could about military affairs, Washington accepted the position. But while Braddock had forty years' service in the king's army and much military experience to impart to the colonials, he was not familiar with warfare in the wilderness. Here, he could learn from Washington and the Virginia troops. But Braddock did not heed their advice as they marched out to confront the French and their Indian allies.

PROVIDENTIAL PROTECTION AT THE
BATTLE OF MONONGAHELA

*W*HEN EDWARD BRADDOCK LAUNCHED his expedition, Washington was ill and too weak to ride a horse, but he was so determined to go along—"which I wou'd not fail in doing . . . for 500 pounds."[51] He rode in a covered wagon at the rear of the army. Washington had tried to warn Braddock that European military tactics would not work in the American frontier, but the general did not listen. His column marched straight into an ambush and was soundly defeated, even though the British and Virginians outnumbered the enemy four to one.[52] Three-quarters of the English officers were killed or wounded;[53] the British regulars abandoned their characteristic calm and order when they encountered the guerrilla tactics of the frontier. Washington wrote, "They behav'd with more cowardice than it is possible to conceive." Only Washington's fearlessness and leadership saved the day. One officer observed that he behaved with "the greatest courage and resolution."[54] Braddock was mortally wounded during the battle. Washington had four bullets pass through his coat and had two horses shot from under him, yet he escaped unhurt.[55] He was fired upon numerous times from near point-blank range and remained unharmed. An Indian chief singled him out and told his warriors to do the same, "but after striving in vain to hit him, [the chief] became alarmed, and told his men to desist from firing at one who was plainly under the care of the great Manitou."[56]

Fifteen years later a chief who took part in this battle made a special effort to visit Washington and spoke to him of this battle and how they attempted to shoot him. The chief said:

> Our rifles were levelled, rifles which, but for him, knew not how to miss—'t was all in vain, a power mightier far than we, shielded him from harm. He can not die in battle. I am old, and soon shall be gathered to the great council-fire of my fathers, in the land of shades, but ere I go, there is a something, bids me speak, in the voice of prophecy. Listen! The Great Spirit protects that man, and guides his destinies—he will become the chief of nations, and a people yet unborn, will hail him as the founder of a mighty empire![57]

In a July 18, 1755, letter to his brother, Washington spoke of God's protection: "As I have heard since my arriv'l at this place, a circumstantial account of my death and dying speech, I take this early oppertunity of contradicting both, and of assuring you that I now exist and appear in the land of the living by the miraculous care of Providence, that protected me beyond all human expectation; I had 4 Bullets through my Coat, and two Horses shot under me, and yet escaped unhurt."[58]

The Reverend Samuel Davies preached a sermon on August 17, 1755, wherein he cited the preservation of Washington. He spoke of "that heroic youth, Colonel Washington, whom I cannot but hope Providence has hitherto preserved in so signal a manner for some important service to his country."[59] In accordance with God's plan, Washington played an extremely important role in the establishment of America as a nation.[60]

Though so ill he could barely sit in the saddle, Washington, as "the only person then left to distribute the Genl's Orders,"[61] led an orderly retreat of what remained of Braddock's army. The British general died three days later and was buried under the road so that his grave could not be found and his body desecrated. Washington himself conducted the funeral service, since no chaplain was present. Before dying, Braddock apologized to Washington for not heeding his advice on how to conduct his campaign.

Washington had lost another battle, but his reputation grew as news of his courage and skill spread throughout the colonies and England. Jared Sparks observes that had the expedition been successful, his superiors would have received all the laurels, but the defeat "should unquestionably be considered as a wise and beneficent dispensation of Providence."[62]

Washington had learned an important lesson: a disciplined army could be defeated by an inferior force. He also learned other lessons taught only by defeat: not to be either too rash or overconfident, to always prepare for the possibility of failure, and to not think too highly of one's own ability. Washington wrote that the survivors of Braddock's expedition had been "most shamefully beaten, by a handful of Men! Who only intended to molest and disturb our march; Victory was their smallest expectation, but see the wondrous works of Providence! The uncertainty of Human things!"[63]

Braddock's defeat brought much fear to those colonists living in western Virginia, due more to marauding Indians than the building of French forts. To address their concerns, the general assembly and Governor Dinwiddie appropriated money for more troops, with Washington as their commander in chief.[64] But Washington faced an impossible job. With only one thousand men, he was responsible for protecting a wild, sparsely populated western border more than 350 miles long that was threatened by a stealthy foe who raided settlements or isolated homes and disappeared into the timber, nearly untraceable. In the end, he proposed construction of a series of forts along the frontier as safe outposts.

Washington's primary task was to form an army from nothing and carry on an impossible campaign with not enough funds or munitions. He faced difficulties in recruiting troops and then organizing, training, and equipping them. His letters and orders reveal his business and organizational skills, great industry, wisdom, and conscientiousness in fulfilling his duty. To compound his difficulties, he was struck with an illness that kept him at Mount Vernon for four months.[65]

Washington expressed great sorrow for the suffering families experienced as a result of Indian raids. He also lamented his inability to do more to alleviate their pain and defeat their enemy. Washington even considered resigning his position, but as everyone looked to him (Speaker John Robinson of the House of Burgesses wrote, "Our hopes, dear George, are all fixed on you"[66]), he persevered in his duty. After he had raised a sufficient force to march on Fort Duquesne, he led them on the difficult march only to find the French had abandoned and burned the fort when they learned that Washington's army was en route. With the Virginians rebuilding and holding the fort, renamed Fort Pitt, the objective of gaining possession of the Ohio River was realized. With this victory and the ensuing decline in Indian raids, after five years in active service, Washington resigned his commission and returned to Mount Vernon, which had suffered during his absence.

These early military experiences revealed many qualities of Washington's character—such as courage, prudence, labor, and sacrifice—and provided opportunities for other qualities to mature—such as confidence and humility. Washington's lifelong belief in God's providence is also evident. In addition, the events of the French and Indian War also gave him experience in the lessons of defeat in battle. In a 1755 letter, he said of himself, "If an old proverb will apply to my case, I shall certainly close with a share of success, for surely no man ever made a worse beginning than I have."[67]

His career as a colonel prepared him for his career as commanding general, encountering many similar situations—raising an army with insufficient funds, lacking adequate support from governing officials, facing great hard-ships and trials on the battlefield, learning how to handle defeat, dealing with unprepared and ill-equipped soldiers, and experiencing the providence of God in protecting his life. Through these events, Washington came to see him-self as an American, not a British subject. He learned the low view the British had of the colonists. He learned that the British army could be defeated by an inferior force, and he learned the tactics necessary to defeat a larger foe. He grew in character, wisdom, and self-reliance. Likewise, his troops respected him greatly. The officers who served under Washington, most of whom were older, wrote: "In you we place the most implicit confidence. Your presence is all that is needed to cause a steady firmness and vigor to actuate in every breast, despising the greatest dangers and thinking light of toils and hardships; while led on by the man we know and love."[68]

No man could have planned future events that would have provided a more beneficial preparation to enable Washington to fulfill his destiny. The hand of Providence is clearly seen in all of this. To not acknowledge it is, to borrow Washington's later words, to be "worse than an infidel that lacks faith, and more than wicked."[69] Washing-ton Irving observed: "In the hand of Heaven he stood to be shaped and trained for its great purpose; and every trial and vicissitude of his early life but fitted him to cope with one or other of the varied and multifarious duties of his fu-ture destiny."[70]

Marriage and Life
as a Virginia Planter

*G*EORGE WASHINGTON WAS INTRODUCED to Martha Custis while he was on his way to Williamsburg in 1758. Her husband had died some time before, leaving her with two children and a large estate. She was attractive, virtuous, wealthy, and a perfect mate for the rising star of Virginia. They were married on January 6, 1759, both nearly twenty-seven years of age. At this time, while well off, Washington was not of the highest plantation class. With Martha's thousands of acres and other holdings added to his already sizable lands, the couple joined the ranks of the richest Virginians. After living three months at her home on the York River, they moved to Mount Vernon and settled down to plantation life.[71]

Martha was very pious. Her grandson, George Washington Parke Custis, said that for fifty years she daily spent time in prayer and reading Scripture.[72] George and Martha had a good relationship that grew stronger over the years. During their forty years of marriage, Washington wrote a number of letters to Martha, but unfortunately only three survive, as he instructed her to burn all of them at his death (such burning of an individual's letters was a common practice in the eighteenth century). Thus there is no resource material to reveal Washington's intimate thoughts with Martha.

For the next fifteen years Washington spent a long season of happiness in private life, a time full of industry, whether in work or play. He exercised his great talents to build up his farms and many businesses. Although he had inherited some land and wealth and gained some by marriage, most of his wealth was acquired and maintained by his labor, business skills, and organization. He took an active role in all aspects of his plantation. He was generally frugal, though he purchased many furnishings, especially in the early 1760s, worth possibly two million dollars (in today's money). He regularly inspected his farms and directly oversaw their operation. In his diary he noted various activities: "Surveyed the water courses of my Mount Vernon tract of land," "Laid off a road from Mount Vernon," "rid to Muddy Hole, Dogue Run and Mill plantation," and so on.

During these years he engineered many changes and innovations. He switched from growing tobacco as a cash crop to planting wheat. He built his own mill to grind the grain and sold flour. He started a fishing business. He was not complacent in going along with the English mercantile system, which kept many planters in debt to their agents in London. He built a new plow, "bottled thirty-five dozen of cider,"[73] and developed a new scientific means of agriculture. One of his goals was to make the land more productive.

These years were also a time of service to others. He adopted Martha's children and acted as their guardian, managing the six-thousand-acre estates they inherited from their father in such a way that they greatly prospered. He oversaw the children's education and advised them on love and many other matters as he prepared them for adulthood. In return, the children loved him greatly.

At the same time, he served in the House of Burgesses for more than fifteen years, beginning in 1759. He also served as a vestryman in the Anglican Church, which was an elected position and required involvement not only in direct church matters but also in many social issues within the parish, including overseeing providing for the poor. He was a faithful church member, regularly observed the Sabbath, and helped build two new church buildings.

Amid all this, Washington enjoyed himself. Foxhunting was his favorite recreational activity. During these plantation years, he averaged a foxhunt every two weeks. There were regular social visits with friends and family as well as many other visitors at Mount Vernon. The Washingtons were very hospitable. George loved dancing, and he was known to dance all night at times. He enjoyed cards, though G. W. P. Custis noted that he played only whist and even gave that up later on.

Washington dressed well, but he was not ostentatious. He ordered many fashions from England for his family and himself. He enjoyed wine at dinner and an occasional stronger drink, but never in excess. He spoke out against drunkenness throughout his life. Everything he did, he did well. Nothing escaped his notice, from worker productivity to the efficiency of farming equipment.

Next to his faith and his family, improving his farms and business was his foremost concern, but he took time to cultivate friendships as well. He did not spend a great amount of time theorizing about philosophical ideas but rather carried on in a steady, methodical way the business then before him, whether that was managing a farm, dancing at a ball, or attending a county meeting or legislative session. He tended his wife through measles, and helped her nurse her daughter Patsy through years of illness. When smallpox broke out among his slaves, he visited them often and did all he could to relieve their affliction.

POLITICAL AFFAIRS

*W*ASHINGTON'S TIME IN THE House of Burgesses introduced him to the leading Virginians of his day and led to his direct involvement in the rising conflict with Britain. In 1765, he heard newly elected delegate Patrick Henry give his famous "If this be treason" speech in response to the passage of the Stamp Act by England, which levied taxes upon the colonists without their consent.[74] In the years that followed, Henry, Washington, and others spoke of the need to resist. Their rights as British subjects, as Christians, and as men were being violated.[75]

The many abuses of their rights, as well as their unsuccessful attempts to have these rectified, were later delineated in the Declaration of Independence. Washington's view that Parliament had no right to tax the colonists without their consent and of the colonists' need to take the next step after their petitions were rejected is seen in a letter to his friend Bryan Fairfax: "What hope then from petitioning, when they tell us, that now or never is the time to fix the matter? Shall we, after this, whine and cry for relief, when we have already tried it in vain? Or shall we supinely sit and see one province after another fall a prey to despotism? . . . I think the Parliament of Great Britain hath no more right to put their hands into my pocket, without my consent, than I have to put my hands into yours for money."[76]

Continued remonstrance was encouraged, but more needed to be done, as was stated in the Fairfax County Resolves, passed on June 18, 1774, at a meeting chaired by Washington. One of the resolves recommended a boycott of British goods. While some were speaking against the tyrannical acts of Parliament, Washington took action. He organized the boycott and stopped purchasing items himself. He believed starving England's trade and manufactures was the best way to get Parliament's attention, and such means should be tried before anyone considered arms or talk of independence.

In the beginning of the opposition to Parliament's actions, there was no talk of independence for the colonies. The colonists saw themselves as British and wished to remain loyal subjects. Benjamin Franklin expressed this mind-set to a British lord some years before, saying that no idea of independence "will ever enter their heads, unless you grossly abuse them."[77]

Another resolve declared, "No slaves ought to be imported into any of the British colonies on this continent; and we take this opportunity of declaring our most earnest wishes to see an entire stop for ever put to such a wicked, cruel and unnatural trade."[78] Britain did not act upon this resolve, but the United States later would, ending the slave trade in America, outlawing slavery in many states, and prohibiting slavery in the Northwest Territory. As was his nature, Washington would take many antislavery actions as well (see pages 161–64, "Washington and Slavery").

In response to the Boston Tea Party in December 1773, Parliament closed the port on June 1, 1774, with the goal of starving the citizens into submission. In response, the Virginia House of Burgesses passed resolutions of sympathy for Boston and declared that June 1 should be set aside "as a Day of Fasting, Humiliation and Prayer, devoutly to implore the divine Interposition" for His aid. The Burgesses were to attend church services on that day for prayer and a sermon. In his diary for that day, Washington recorded: "Went to Church & fasted all day."[79] Washington not only gave spiritual support to Massachusetts but also financial support, contributing fifty pounds toward their relief in one of the collections that occurred throughout the states.

In August 1774, the House of Burgesses selected seven members—including Washington and Henry—to attend the first meeting of representatives from all of the colonies, which gathered in Philadelphia. The First Continental Congress convened the next month. One of its first acts was to call for a minister to open their proceedings in prayer. In a letter to his wife, John Adams described the great effect that the Reverend Jacob Duché's prayer had upon the Congress.[80] When Henry was asked who was the greatest man in this Congress he replied: "If you speak of eloquence, Mr. [John] Rutledge, of South Carolina, is by far the greatest orator; but if you speak of solid information and sound judgment, Colonel Washington is unquestionably the greatest man on that floor."[81]

By March 1775, many colonial leaders saw that they must begin to prepare militarily for a defensive war. Patrick Henry introduced a resolution to the Virginia legislature, then meeting in Richmond at St. John's Church, to authorize the counties to form local militias. When opposition arose from some delegates who feared retribution from England, Henry delivered his famous "Give me liberty or give me death" speech. He declared, "An appeal to arms and to the God of Hosts is all that is left us!"[82] With Washington's support, this measure passed. Not content with resolutions alone, Washington pledged to raise an army of a thousand men himself. Others may have led the way with words, but Washington took the lead with his actions.

After the colonists were fired upon at Lexington and Concord in April 1775, they had no choice but to defend themselves. Washington wrote: "That the Americans will fight for their Liberties and property, however pusilanimous, in his Lordship's Eye, they may appear in other respects. . . . Unhappy it is though to reflect, that a Brother's Sword has been sheathed in a Brother's breast, and that, the once happy and peaceful plains of America are either to be drenched with Blood, or Inhabited by Slaves. Sad alternative! But can a virtuous Man hesitate in his choice?"[83]

GENERAL OF THE
CONTINENTAL ARMY

*A*S EVENTS PROGRESSED AND war became imminent, Washington prepared for his military
role by ordering some books on tactics and obtaining new
uniforms. When he traveled to the Second Continental
Congress as a member of the Virginia delegation, he took
his uniform. He must have had an idea that he might be
appointed to some leadership position. Certainly, most of
the delegates knew he would be the best choice for general of the armies. On June 15, Washington was unanimously elected as commander in chief, which Adams said
would "have a great Effect, in cementing and securing the
Union of these Colonies."[84]

While other men had more military experience than
Washington, none had more experience in organizing an
army from scratch, training those who had no military
background, outfitting an army despite insufficient funds,

governing self-sufficient men, and overcoming the many difficulties arising from governing officials seeking too much control of military affairs. He had faced all these problems earlier, during the French and Indian War. Washington had the experience, but he also had the character to deal with these challenges.

His motive for accepting the position was not personal aggrandizement, for he had much to lose. The chance of victory was small. If the colonists lost, he would be seen as a leader of the rebellion and likely hanged. At the least, his land and possessions would have been confiscated, his reputation lost, his family thrown into disarray, and their lives and liberties put in jeopardy. He would lose his public standing, his fortune, and most everything he had built up since early manhood.

He wrote of his reluctance: "Tho' I am truly sensible of the high Honour done me in this Appointment, yet I feel great distress from a consciousness that my abilities and Military experience may not be equal to the extensive and important Trust. . . . I this day declare with the utmost sincerity, I do not think my self equal to the Command I am honoured with."[85]

He did not think he was up to the job, and he was right. No one would have been up to the task of organizing an army comprising laborers and farmers to battle the greatest military force in the world. He had some experience, but he lacked much more than he had.

While he was not qualified for the job, nonetheless, he was willing to respond to the call of duty, to do all he could for the "glorious Cause." Thus he concluded, "However, as the Congress desires I will enter upon the momentous duty, and exert every power I Possess In their Service for the Support of the glorious Cause."[86] He said he would serve without pay, as no amount of money could convince him to assume this role.[87] He expressed the same motives of duty and service in private correspondence to Martha, his stepson, and his brother-in-law (see pages 234–39, "Humility and Modesty").

George wrote Martha of his appointment, explaining that he had to go immediately to Massachusetts to assume command of the army. He added: "I shall rely, therefore, confidently on that Providence, which has heretofore preserved and been bountiful to me, not doubting but that I shall return safe to you in the fall."[88] While he did return safe, it was not in the fall. In fact, more than six years passed before he saw Mount Vernon again. He did see Martha, though, as she stayed with him during winter encampments, when the armies refrained from campaigning.

Washington arrived in Watertown, Massachusetts, on July 2, where he was officially welcomed by a delegation. The welcome concluded: "We most fervently implore Almighty God, that the blessings of Divine Providence may rest on you; that your head may be covered in the day of battle; that every necessary assistance may be afforded; and that you may be long continued in life and health, a blessing to mankind."[89]

The people here, as throughout the colonies, were praying for his army's success. These prayers, coupled with his own, are what sustained Washington and eventually brought about the successful conclusion of the war.

Washington assumed command of the troops at Cambridge on July 3. He was easily recognized among the entourage that rode up to review the troops assembled. George Thatcher wrote: "It was not difficult to distinguish him from all others. He is tall and well-proportioned, and his personal appearance truly noble and majestic."[90]

Washington immediately began the task of organizing the army, despite inadequate supplies, tents, ammunition, or money and with few skilled officers to assist in the necessary training. He had only raw recruits, men who had never worked for another. And this nearly impossible feat had to be done within sight of a well-stocked, well-armed, and well-disciplined army.

Washington's first orders, issued on July 4, reflect those things he considered as basic for a successful army and communicated to the troops his character and expectations. After stating the need for discipline and subordination among the army, his orders forbade "profane cursing, swearing, and drunkenness," and when not on duty required "a punctual attendance on divine Service, to implore the blessing of heaven upon the means used for our safety and defence."[91]

Washington was cautious to engage the enemy, as immediate defeat could likely mean the end of the war, but he also saw that his army was in a favorable situation to engage the enemy directly, and if he were victorious, the Continentals could possibly realize their objectives with no further fighting. He presented two different plans to his war council to attack Boston directly, but after taking their counsel, he realized the risks were too great, and thus he assumed a more cautious attitude. His inaction brought criticism from some, but duty, not public opinion, guided him at this time and throughout the entire war. In the end, he planned to surround Boston and prepare for any assault the British might mount; then he would push his lines forward until his cannon were within range to fire into the city and thus force the British to withdraw their army and navy. This strategy required patience and time, which caused great concern for Washington. He wrote to the president of Congress: "My Situation is expressibly distressing to see the Winter fast approaching upon a naked Army, The time of their Service within a few Weeks of expiring, and no Provision yet made for such important Events. Added to this the Military Chest is totally exhausted."[92] Ammunition was in short supply—"not powder enough in the whole camp for nine cartridges to a man."[93] Few men had blankets, many were sick, many complained of inactivity, and most said they would leave as soon as their short enlistment expired. Washington had to deal with individual militia groups, each having enlisted for different lengths of time and with different expectations.

He had faced such hardships twenty years before, though failure now would result in much graver consequences. The great burden of leadership fell heavily upon Washington. Though seldom displayed in his public letters, his feelings were at times expressed to his friends. To Joseph Reed, he wrote:

> Few people know the predicament we are in. . . . I have often thought how much happier I should have been, if, instead of accepting of a command under such circumstances, I had taken my musket on my shoulder and entered the ranks, or, if I could have justified the measure to posterity and my own conscience, had retired to the back

country, and lived in a wigwam. If I shall be able to rise superior to these and many other difficulties, which might be enumerated, I shall most religiously believe, that the finger of Providence is in it, to blind the eyes of our enemies; for surely if we get well through this month, it must be for want of their knowing the disadvantages we labour under.[94]

Washington and his army overcame their many difficulties. His strategy of erecting a fortification on Dorchester Hill in a single night, thus being able to fire directly upon the British, forced the evacuation of the city. The industry and skill of the Continental army was such that British Gen. William Howe said, "The rebels have done more in a single night than my whole army would have done in a month."[95] The accomplishment was perceived as miraculous, as one officer wrote of the erected works, "They were raised with an expedition equal to that of the Genii belonging to Aladdin's Wonderful Lamp."[96] Not the finger of a genie, but the finger of Providence was in it, and Washington acknowledged he had been "an instrument in the late signal interposition of Providence."[97] Eighty-nine hundred British troops departed the city in seventy-eight ships and transports on March 17, 1776. Not long after this, Washington responded to an address from the Massachusetts legislature: "Its [the evacuation] being effected without the blood of our soldiers and fellow-citizens must be ascribed to the interposition of that Providence, which has manifestly appeared in our behalf through the whole of this important struggle. . . . May that being, who is powerful to save, and in whose hands is the fate of nations, look down with an eye of tender pity and compassion upon the whole of the United Colonies; may He continue to smile upon their counsels and arms, and crown them with success, whilst employed in the cause of virtue and mankind."[98]

As he had done previously, the man of Providence acknowledged the superintending care of God in the events in history—events that were central, not just to the future of a small colony in New England, but in the advancement of liberty for all mankind—and petitioned God's continued aid.

On the same day the British evacuated Boston, Washington and some of his officers attended a thanksgiving service where the Reverend Abiel Leonard preached a sermon based on Exodus 14:25: "And [they] took off their chariot wheels, that they drave them heavily: so that the Egyptians said, Let us flee from the face of Israel; for the LORD fighteth for them against the Egyptians."[99] In addition to attending Sunday meetings when the circumstances allowed, Washington attended special thanksgiving and fast day sermons throughout the war. Many of these were held in conjunction with colony-wide days of prayer proclaimed by the Continental Congress, which were recognized at least thirteen times during the war. Other special services were held on the days of prayer proclaimed by state assemblies and governors, which were numerous.[100]

Due to an agreement between Howe and Washington, Boston was not put to the torch when the British left, but the one-year British occupation of Boston did not endear the British to the American people. They had commandeered many homes, thus sparking the grievance in the Declaration of "quartering large bodies of armed troops among us." They profaned places of worship, including stabling horses in the Old South Meeting House; another church and three hundred homes were torn down and the timber used for fuel. Trade came to a standstill, depriving the citizens of basic necessities. Despite the agreement between the generals, as Howe's troops evacuated the city, they seized property, robbed stores and ships, and defaced property. Other states during the war experienced the same behavior when the British occupied and then withdrew from their areas.

Washington's patient strategy regained the city of Boston without resorting to a direct assault, which would have resulted in many casualties. Praise came from many sources, including Congress, who ordered a gold medal be struck with Washington's image on one side. Washington responded with characteristic modesty, saying he had only done his duty and he hoped the outcome would contribute to freedom and peace.

Howe's army sailed to New York, and Washington led his army there to confront them again. During the spring and summer, the Americans prepared fortifications as British ships collected in the harbor. When Washington received the Declaration of Independence from Congress, he ordered that it be read aloud to the troops with the hope of inspiring them "to act with Fidelity and Courage, as knowing that now the peace and safety of his Country depends (under God) solely on the success of our arms."[101]

In these same orders of July 9, 1776, Washington indicated that Congress had approved the hiring of chaplains for the army. So he directed his commanders "to procure Chaplains accordingly; persons of good Characters and exemplary lives." The troops and officers were to respect them and "attend carefully upon religious exercises. The blessing and protection of Heaven are at all times necessary but especially so in times of public distress and danger—The General hopes and trusts, that every officer and man, will endeavour so to live, and act, as becomes a Christian Soldier defending the dearest Rights and Liberties of his country."[102]

Toward the end of August 1776, British forces landed on Long Island. Not long thereafter a battle ensued, with Continental troops sent over from New York City to meet them. In the initial conflict, the greatly outnumbered Continentals lost about eleven hundred men, either killed, wounded, or captured. Washington himself was awake forty-eight consecutive hours and almost continually on his horse.[103] At one point in the battle, Washington observed the troops under William Alexander (Lord Stirling) attack a much superior force with no hope of victory. At this sight, he declared in agony, "Good God, what brave fellows I must this day lose!"[104] The extraordinary retreat across the East River that followed was one of the most improbable and important events of the war, which many attributed to "a peculiar Providence"[105] (see pages 174–83, "The Providence of God").

In the weeks that followed, the situation of the Continental army was "truly distressing"[106] from both internal challenges and attacks from British ships and troops at various sites around New York. One observer wrote that three men were killed by a cannonball and that "one shot struck within six feet of General Washington, as he was on horseback, riding into the fort."[107] This was one of many close encounters Washington had with enemy fire during the war. His preservation from harm was attributed to the protection of Providence.

After continued setbacks and the capture of Fort Washington by the British, Washington retreated to New Jersey. As he was outnumbered by the British troops who pursued him, Washington did not believe it prudent to directly engage the enemy. His army amounted to about four thousand men, and sickness reduced by one-quarter those who could fight. His defensive policies brought charges of incompetence from some, yet Washington chose not to address his critics because he did not want to expose his weakness to the enemy.

As 1776 drew to a close, Washington had been chased through New Jersey and into Pennsylvania. A continual string of failures threatened the resolve of the army and the American people. Added to all his problems, Continental Gen. Charles Lee chose not to respond to Washington's orders in a timely manner and secretly undermined his authority, seeking to replace Washington as commander in chief. Others had joined Lee in believing a change was needed. But while Lee was complaining of Washington's incompetence, Lee was captured as a result of his own incompetence. The British boasted of capturing this great prize, since Lee was second in command of the Continental army, but they more probably providentially assisted the American cause by removing the one man who might have supplanted Washington as general in chief.

While the problem with Lee was gone, the dire situation facing the American cause remained. The British marched where they chose, looking as if they would take over Philadelphia and winter there. Washington could do little to stop them because his army had continued to shrink, and at year's end, the enlistments of many more would expire. If more men did not join or if something did not occur to rally the nation, Washington wrote, "I think the game will be pretty well up," as he believed the colonists did not have the fortitude to continue the resistance.[108]

"This was the gloomiest period of the war," Jared Sparks observed,[109] yet, even so, Washington stood firm and positive under all the pressure and great hardships. When asked what he would do if Philadelphia was taken by the enemy, he said, "We will retreat beyond the Susquehanna River; and thence, if necessary, to the Alleghany Mountains."[110] Washington wrote to his brother, "No man, I believe, ever had a greater choice of difficulties and less means to extricate himself from them." However, believing in "the justice of our Cause I cannot but think the prospect will brighten," though at the time it was "hid under a cloud."[111] For the prospect to brighten, something had to happen: he planned a bold surprise attack on the Hessian garrison at Trenton.

On the evening of December 25, Continental troops began crossing the Delaware River. Washington led twenty-four hundred men from the north, with plans of meeting up with troops marching from the south. Severe weather and much ice in the river delayed Washington by many hours; the other troops were not able to cross. After landing they marched nine miles through snow and sleet to surprise the Hessians (German mercenaries hired by the

British). After a brief resistance, in which thirty-two died in the fighting, about a thousand troops surrendered to the Continentals, who suffered no casualties in the fighting, although two had died during the march.[112] Not long after this, the "old fox" Washington eluded a larger British army sent to engage him at Trenton, and he garnered a victory on January 3 at Princeton. These two triumphs between December 25, 1776, and January 4, 1777, were, according to Frederick the Great of Prussia, "the most brilliant of any in the annals of military achievements."[113] British Gen. Charles Cornwallis, after his defeat at Yorktown, later said to Washington: "And when the illustrious part that your excellency has borne in this long and arduous contest becomes a matter of history, fame will gather our brightest laurels from the banks of the Delaware than from those of the Chesapeake."[114]

These twin victories were a great boost to the morale of the army and the colonists and helped elevate Washington in the eyes of the people. Past failures were forgotten, and the people spoke only of Washington's wisdom and patience. Within three weeks, he had dislodged the British from all their posts on the Delaware River and from all but two in New Jersey; he had driven away despondency, revived the martial spirit, and renewed hope that liberty was not lost. Not only Americans but many from other nations began to declare Washington as the savior of his country.[115]

The year 1777 began well with the victory at Princeton and included a few more encouraging events, one being the arrival of the Marquis de Lafayette. He was a friend to liberty and become a close friend and important officer to

Washington. But as the year progressed, the Continental army suffered defeats in September at Brandywine and in the first week of October at Germantown, enabling the British to occupy Philadelphia and drive the Continental Congress from the city. Though suffering about a thousand casualties, Washington's army nearly gained a victory at Germantown. The general's attack at Germantown may have even contributed to France's becoming an ally of the Continentals.[116]

On October 7, 1777, Washington ordered the army's chaplains to ensure they regularly conducted services since their situation did not always allow them to do so on Sundays. In light of the army's recent losses, this reveals the importance Washington placed on worship.

Not long after this, one of the most important events of the war occurred—British Gen. John Burgoyne surrendered on October 17 at Saratoga. Washington called it a "signal stroke of Providence."[117] This battle has been called one of the seven most significant battles in history, because once France learned of this triumph, they saw that their longtime enemy might be defeated, and thus Louis XVI decided to ally with the colonies in the war. French support in terms of troops, munitions, ships, and money was invaluable to the American cause.

In order to remain near the British army in Philadelphia, Washington chose to quarter his troops for the winter at Valley Forge. His situation was desperate in December 1777. Going into the winter camp, the soldiers were hungry, ill clothed, many were shoeless—their marches could be traced by the bloody footprints left in the snow[118]—and many were sick. They also had to prepare for a harsh winter within striking distance of a well-supplied enemy who was nicely accommodated by all that the city of Philadelphia had to offer. Even so, Washington's optimism and faith in God and the cause of liberty continued as strong as ever. In his orders for December 17, 1777, issued while the army was still marching to Valley Forge, he told the troops: "Altho' in some instances we unfortunately failed, yet upon the whole Heaven hath smiled on our Arms and crowned them with signal success; and we may upon the best grounds conclude, that by a spirited continuance of the measures necessary for our defence we shall finally obtain the end of our Warfare, Independence, Liberty and Peace."[119]

As a consequence of the victory at Saratoga, Congress proclaimed December 18, 1777, a day of thanksgiving and praise to God, stating, "It is the indispensable duty of all men to adore the superintending providence of Almighty God, . . . and it having pleased Him in His abundant mercy . . . to crown our arms with most signal success." They recommended all the colonists set aside a day for thanksgiving and praise to confess their sins and humbly ask God, "through the merits of Jesus Christ, mercifully to forgive and blot them out of remembrances" and thus He then would be able to pour out His blessings upon the colonies.[120]

Washington, as he did throughout the war, issued orders for his troops to observe the congressional proclamation: "To morrow being the day set apart by the Honorable Congress for public Thanksgiving and Praise; and duty calling us devoutely to express our grateful acknowledgements to God for the manifold blessings he has granted us.

The General directs . . . that the Chaplains perform divine service with their several Corps and brigades. And earnestly exhorts, all officers and soldiers, whose absence is not indispensibly necessary, to attend with reverence the solemnities of the day."[121]

Added to the immense problems he faced that winter at Valley Forge (see pages 165–73, "Christian Character and Morality," for more on these hardships), Washington also had to address a powerful cabal against him headed by Gens. Thomas Conway and Thomas Mifflin. Their interest in replacing him as commander in chief sprang in part from his failure to keep the British out of Philadelphia. He never expected an easy time. As Washington had written to Lafayette, "We must not, in so great a contest, expect to meet with nothing but Sun shine."[122] However, more than human strength was necessary to survive the numerous obstacles during the war and to achieve victory. Washington must have known this, which is why he spent so much time in prayer during the war, especially during the winter in Valley Forge.

Numerous paintings and drawings over the years depict Washington on his knees in prayer at Valley Forge. There is a stained-glass image of the general thus praying in the prayer room of the U.S. Capitol. Statues also portray this act.

Many writers have recounted the story of Isaac Potts's observing the general in prayer in a secluded grove of trees near his home (see page 171 for Potts's story).[123] Dr. N. R. Snowden and his son reported that Potts pointed out to them "the spot where he saw General Washington at prayer in the winter of 1777. This event induced

Friend Potts to become a Whig; and he told his wife Betty, that the cause of America was a good cause, and would prevail."[124]

Many others in addition to Potts observed Washington in prayer during this time, including Gen. Henry Knox.[125] This scene has inspired many over the past two centuries. On May 6, 1982, President Ronald Reagan remarked on this event in his National Day of Prayer Proclamation: "The most sublime picture in American history is of George Washington on his knees in the snow at Valley Forge. That image personifies a people who know that it is not enough to depend on our own courage and goodness; we must also seek help from God, our Father and Preserver."

Thanks to Washington's leadership and God's superintending care, the army survived Valley Forge, the crucible of freedom. But the army did more than just survive: it marched out of Valley Forge as an army in the truest sense of the word. The hardships the troops endured together, the military training of the Prussian Friedrich von Steuben, and Washington's renewed commitment instilled a strength and confidence in the Continentals that stayed with them throughout the remaining years of the war. Whenever Washington had an important task at hand, he looked for a man who had marched with him to and from Valley Forge.

British troops departed Philadelphia in June 1778 for New York. The Continental army engaged them at Monmouth, New Jersey, on June 28. Gen. Charles Lee, back with the army after a prisoner exchange, was assigned to lead one division, though he had opposed any attack. Contrary to Washington's instructions, Lee ordered his men to retreat when they came under heavy fire. When Washington encountered Lee and his fleeing troops, he lost his temper—one of the few times he did so in public—assumed command in the field, and rallied the troops, all the while exposed to enemy fire (see pages 184–87, "Self-Government").[126] The day ended as a standoff, though it could have been a great failure for the colonials if not for Washington. He believed the fighting would resume the next morning, so he had his troops sleep with their weapons on the battlefield, where he also slept. But during the night, British Gen. Henry Clinton withdrew his army, and the battle was not resumed. Though Monmouth was not considered an outright victory for Washington's troops, the result reflected positively on the Continental army.

In mid-July, about five months after the treaty aligning the American colonies and France had been signed in Paris, a fleet of French ships under the command of the comte d'Estaing arrived in America. Since the Continentals had no navy, this was an important and welcome occurrence. Washington immediately began to coordinate with d'Estaing joint efforts against the British. Their initial actions were not too successful, but the French fleet came to play a vital part in the outcome of the war. D'Estaing's letter of introduction reveals the elevated position that Washington had achieved in the eyes of the world: "The talents and great actions of General Washington have secured to him, in the eyes of all Europe, the truly sublime title of the liberator of America."[127]

Washington continued to state clearly what enabled him to be such a liberator. In an August 20, 1778, letter to

Gen. Thomas Nelson of Virginia, he wrote in the context of contemplating the events of the prior two years: "The hand of Providence has been so conspicuous in all of this, that he must be worse than an infidel that lacks faith, and more than wicked, that has not gratitude enough to acknowledge his obligations, but, it will be time enough for me to turn preacher, when my present appointment ceases; and therefore, I shall add no more on the Doctrine of Providence."[128]

By the end of 1778, the most eminent men were no longer in Congress but in their various states, writing constitutions and serving in state leadership. This not only made Washington's job more difficult but posed a great threat to their united cause. He wrote that the nation should be the first concern of everyone, because if it was not, the Continentals could lose the war, and then the states would have no use for their new governments.[129]

The British committed many atrocities in 1779—plundering property, burning houses, schools, shops, and churches, and encouraging Indians on the frontier to massacre the colonists.[130] But such terror tactics only increased the resolve of the Americans to fight. An expeditionary force was sent to the frontier to deal with the Indians, and Washington's army assumed a defensive posture. As winter approached, Washington set up his headquarters at Morristown, New Jersey. The most severe winter of the war was yet to come.

Obtaining the necessary food, supplies, arms, and money to sustain the army was a constant challenge for Washington. Powerless to raise funds directly, Congress had issued currency to pay for the war, but this paper money became almost worthless over time, hence the expression "not worth a continental." Washington appealed to the states, business leaders, local farmers and merchants, and all Americans to help, and many came to his aid. Several ladies' associations formed in the different states to collect money for the army. Washington also begged them to furnish shirts. In 1780 he wrote that he admired "the patriotic spirit of the Ladies of Philadelphia" for their "benevolent and generous donation" and suggested they use the funds to buy shirts, "a supply of eight or ten thousand," if funds permitted.[131]

His troops also lacked food. Urgently and often he wrote to Congress and the states pleading for assistance, explaining that his men as well as his officers were at times "almost perishing for want, alternately without bread or meat, with a very scanty allowance of either—frequently destitute of both. . . . Our affairs are in so deplorable a condition on the score of provisions, as to fill the mind with the most anxious fears. Men half-starved, imperfectly clothed, and robbing the country people of their subsistence from sheer necessity."[132]

Despite the great difficulties of the war, Washington did not despair. A belief in the cause and the overruling providence of God gave him hope the Continentals would eventually succeed. God seemed to always come to their aid.

DISCOVERY OF
BENEDICT ARNOLD'S TREASON

*I*N SEPTEMBER 1780 "a combination of extraordinary circumstances"[133] occurred that led to the capture of British Maj. John André and the discovery of Benedict Arnold's plan to yield West Point to the British. Washington explained what happened in a letter to Gen. William Heath:

> Major General Arnold has gone to the Enemy. He had had an interview with Major Andre, Adjutant Genl. of the British Army, and had put into his possession a state of our Army; of the Garrison at this post; . . . By a most providential interposition, Major Andre was taken in returning to New York with all these papers in General Arnold's hand writing, who hearing of the matter kept it secret, left his Quarters immediately under pretence of going over to West point on Monday forenoon, . . . then pushed down

the river in the barge, which was not discovered till I had returned from West point in the Afternoon.[134]

After André had met with Arnold and obtained the information, he was traveling back to New York in civilian dress to deliver it to his superiors. On the road, he encountered a few American militiamen whom he mistook for loyalists. He talked too freely, which aroused their suspicion. They searched André and found the incriminating papers in his stockings. "They were offered," Washington wrote, "a large sum of money for his release, and as many goods as they would demand, but without effect. Their conduct gives them a just claim to the thanks of their country."[135] The militiamen took André to the nearest military outpost, where the officer, not realizing Arnold's participation in the plot, notified him of André's capture. Thus warned, Arnold fled to British lines. Had his treasonous plans not been found out, West Point would have fallen into British hands, which would have been a blow too great for the Continentals to sustain.

Washington wrote to Lt. Col. John Laurens, "In no instance since the commencement of the War has the interposition of Providence appeared more conspicuous than in the rescue of the Post and Garrison of West point from Arnolds villainous perfidy."[136] In his general orders for September 26, 1780, Washington declared: "Treason of the blackest dye was yesterday discovered! General Arnold who commanded at Westpoint, lost to every sentiment of honor, of public and private obligation, was about to deliver up that important Post into the hands of the enemy. Such an event must have given the American cause a deadly wound if not a fatal stab. Happily the treason has been timely discovered to prevent the fatal misfortune. The providential train of circumstances which led to it affords the most convincing proof that the Liberties of America are the object of divine Protection."[137]

The Continental Congress also attributed the discovery of the treason to "Almighty God, the Father of all mercies." They "recommended to the several states to set apart Thursday, the seventh day of December next, to be observed as a day of public thanksgiving and prayer" where the people should praise and thank God, ask Him to pardon their sins and to smile upon their endeavors, petition Him for peace and blessings, and "to cause the knowledge of Christianity to spread over all the earth."[138]

André was convicted and sentenced to death. Since he acted honorably, Washington hoped to spare him by exchanging him for Arnold, but the British would not agree to this and so, Washington wrote, "Andre has met his fate, and with that fortitude which was to be expected from an accomplished man, and gallant officer. But I am mistaken, if at this time, Arnold is undergoing the torments of a mental Hell."[139]

In 1780 and 1781 much of the war shifted to the southern colonies, with battles at Charlestown, Cowpens, and Guilford Courthouse. Benedict Arnold, now leading British forces, ravaged Virginia towns that were helpless to defend themselves. A British man-of-war sailed up the Potomac River and halted at Mount Vernon, demanding supplies from Lund Washington (a distant cousin of the general), the manager of Mount Vernon, as the price for sparing the general's house and property. Not wanting to see everything destroyed, he complied. This brought a strong rebuke from the general, who said he would rather have seen the house burned and everything destroyed rather than aid the enemy.

By mid-1781, British Gen. Charles Cornwallis had entered Virginia from the south and was positioning his troops on the York River to link up with the British fleet that would be sailing from New York. Washington dispatched Lafayette to counteract Cornwallis's actions in Virginia while he considered an assault against New York with the combined French and Continental armies. When he learned that the French fleet under comte de Grasse would be sailing from the West Indies to the Chesapeake, he decided to march to Yorktown, disguising his movements so that British Gen. Henry Clinton in New York would not realize his intent until it was too late. The comte de Rochambeau also led his army to Yorktown.

On the way to meet up with Lafayette near Williamsburg, Washington and Rochambeau stopped at Mount Vernon. This was Washington's first visit to his beloved home in more than six years, and the stay was very brief.

Surrender at Yorktown

*B*Y THE FIRST PART of October, Washington had surrounded the British in their fortified position in Yorktown and shortly thereafter began the attack.[140] The British fleet sent to relieve Cornwallis never made it; the French fleet arrived at the mouth of the Chesapeake Bay in time to force the British ships to return to New York. Without reinforcements, Cornwallis briefly held out against the siege of the Continental and French forces. As a last resort, he decided to retreat across the York River. At ten o'clock on the night of October 17, sixteen boats were loaded with troops and embarked for Gloucester. After the first few boats had landed, the situation suddenly changed. In his report of what happened at Yorktown, Cornwallis wrote: "But at this critical moment, the weather, from being moderate and calm, changed to a violent storm of wind and rain, and drove all the boats, some of which had troops on board, down the river."[141] Due to this miraculous change in the weather, Cornwallis was unable to complete his withdrawal and found his army divided when Washington's batteries opened fire at daybreak. When the boats finally returned, the British commander ordered them to bring back the troops that had been delivered to the opposite shore during the night. Later that day, he surrendered his forces to Washington. This essentially marked the end of the war.

Washington and the Continental Congress recognized the providence of God in the battle of Yorktown. The *Journals of the Continental Congress* record: "Resolved, that Congress will, at two o'clock this day, go in procession to the Dutch Lutheran Church, and return thanks to Almighty God, for crowning the allied arms of the United States and France, with success, by the surrender of the Earl of Cornwall."[142]

In his congratulatory order to the allied army on the day after the official surrender on October 19, Washington wrote: "The General congratulates the Army upon the glorious event of yesterday. . . . Divine Service is to be performed tomorrow in the several Brigades or Divisions. The Commander in Chief earnestly recommends that the troops not on duty should universally attend with that seriousness of Deportment and gratitude of Heart which the recognition of such reiterated and astonishing interpositions of Providence demand of us."[143]

Not long after the surrender of Cornwallis, Washington's joy was tempered by news that his twenty-eight-year-old stepson, Jackie Custis, lay dying of a fever in a friend's home in Eltham, attended by Martha and Jackie's

wife, Nelly. Upon arriving and learning of Jackie's imminent death, Washington wept profusely.

Jackie and Nelly had four small children. At Jackie's
deathbed, Washington promised to be a father to them. He
and Martha adopted the two youngest and raised them as
their own. The daughter, Eleanor Parke Custis, later married Lawrence Lewis, Washington's favorite nephew. The
son, George Washington Parke Custis, went on to build
Arlington, just across the Potomac River from what would
become the national capital, as a museum to George
Washington. Wanting to perpetuate the memory of Washington, Custis invited people to his home to see the memo-
rabilia. His daughter Mary would marry Robert E. Lee in
1831 and live at the estate off and on until the Civil War
began. The home still stands today in the middle of Arlington National Cemetery and is known as the Arlington
House or R. E. Lee Memorial.

Yorktown was the last major battle of the war, but it
would be almost two years before the treaty ending the
war was signed. During negotiations, Washington had to
maintain the army in case the British resolved to resume
the fighting. Thus the hardships of the army continued:
lack of pay, food, and clothing. A number of officers believed Congress would never be able to deal with the problems of the army or of the newly formed United States.
They were aware that up to that time, the English constitutional monarchy had proved to be the most successful
form of government. With this as their model, in May
1782 some officers proposed making Washington king of
the new country. His reply shows his great character (see
pages 165–73, "Christian Character and Morality") and

ensured the opportunity for a new form of civil government to come forth—a self-governed republic.

About a year later, with no improvement in conditions,
many officers decided to take matters into their own
hands. A meeting was planned to discuss a military coup.
Washington learned of this unsanctioned gathering of officers and called his own meeting to persuade them not to
pursue this drastic action. His example and Christian
character again thwarted what could have ended the new
experiment in liberty just beginning in America (see pages
203–8, "Duty and Service").

PEACE AND THE
FRUITS OF VICTORY

A PRELIMINARY TREATY OF peace between the
United States and Great Britain was signed
in Paris on November 30, 1782. On April 19, 1783, eight
years after the battle of Lexington, this proclamation ending hostilities was read to the army, after which, in accordance with Washington's orders, the troops attended
divine service and heard prayers of thanksgiving from the
chaplains. They thanked almighty God for His mercies,
"particularly for his over ruling the wrath of man to his
own glory, and causing the rage of war to cease among
nations."[144]

England recognized the independence of the United
States in the final treaty, which was signed in Paris on September 3, 1783. Independence had finally been won, but
not without great sacrifice. None had given more than
Washington, but he only considered it his duty and

looked for no reward nor even thanks. But thanks and adulations were poured upon him from all over America and the world.

In preparation for disbanding the army, Washington wrote a farewell to his troops, reiterating a familiar theme: "The singular interpositions of Providence in our feeble condition were such, as could scarcely escape the attention of the most unobserving." He reminded his soldiers to display their virtues in civilian life just as they had in military life: "The private virtues of economy, prudence, and industry, will not be less amiable in civil life, than the more splendid qualities of valor, perseverance and enterprise were in the field."[145] Such character was needed in all the people of the United States for the nation to survive and progress. He expressed similar ideas to the governors of the states in the summer of 1783. In what he considered to be his last public counsel, he communicated a number of important points he believed necessary for the support of the new nation. Foremost was a strong indissoluble union; thus, he encouraged friendly relations between the states. He spoke of the need for public justice, "the adoption of a proper Peace Establishment," and public and private virtue that would be supplied by living in accordance with the Christian faith. He concluded his "Circular to the Governors of the States" with a prayer:

> I now make it my earnest prayer, that God would have you, and the State over which you preside, in his holy protection, that he would incline the hearts of the Citizens to cultivate a spirit of subordination and obedience to Government, to entertain a brotherly affection and

love for one another, for their fellow Citizens of the United States at large, and particularly for their brethren who have served in the Field, and finally, that he would most graciously be pleased to dispose us all, to do Justice, to love mercy, and to demean ourselves with that Charity, humility, and pacific temper of mind, which were the Characteristics of the Divine Author of our blessed Religion, and without an humble imitation of whose example in these things, we can never hope to be a happy Nation.[146]

Toward the end of November, the last British troops departed New York City, after which U.S. forces, Washington, and various officials entered the city and celebrated. On December 4 Washington gave a final farewell to his officers at Fraunces Tavern. With much emotion and many tears, Washington took each of his principal officers by the hand after toasting: "I most devoutly wish, that your latter days may be as prosperous and happy, as your former ones have been glorious and honorable."[147]

Washington then traveled to Annapolis to meet with Congress and resign his commission as commander in chief. He now assumed the role of Cincinnatus as he gladly returned to Mount Vernon to take up "the plow and the pruning knife," which was far more dear to him than any wreaths of victory obtained by the sword. His action assured civilian control of the military in the United States. Unlike many other nations throughout history, America's revolution did not end with military rule, nor has America experienced a military coup. Washington's character and example set those precedents.

The result of American victory in the Revolution was the beginning of a new era of liberty in history. America was unique among the nations. She was unique in her founding principles. The people who formed her covenant recognized that all men are created equal, that they have Creator-endowed rights to life, liberty, and property; such rights are not government granted. They recognized governments exist to serve man, not vice versa, and that man is superior to the state. They appealed to "the Supreme judge of the world" for their support and acknowledged their reliance upon "divine Providence." They had established a republic based upon self-governed individuals. However, the success of the American republic was far from certain. She would need a new form of government just as remarkable as her founding principles in order to provide a framework for liberty to grow and the nation to prosper. While the American Cincinnatus was satisfied to live out his days at home, his nation once again would have need of his services, and he would respond to this duty with the same humility and sense of service that he had displayed before.

With the victorious end of the war, George Washington became the most famous person in the world. Many people in many nations spoke of him. Frederick the Great of Prussia was a great admirer. He sent him a sword with the message, "from the oldest general in Europe to the greatest in the world."[148] Though Washington's fame grew great, he did not seek praise nor speak of his accomplishments. As he did throughout the war, he acknowledged that his success was due to God, and to Him alone was the praise due. Responding to a letter of congratulations on his victory in the Revolution, Washington wrote, "Glorious indeed has been our Contest: glorious, if we consider the Prize for which we have contended, and glorious in its Issue; but in the midst of our Joys, I hope we shall not forget that, to divine Providence is to be ascribed the Glory and the Praise."[149]

Private Life at Mount Vernon

*A*FTER RESIGNING HIS COMMISSION as commander in chief, Washington retired to his beloved Mount Vernon believing his public career was ended. He had been gone from his home for eight and a half years, making only two short stops there on his way to and from Yorktown in 1781. He was now ready to devote himself to that which he enjoyed the most: improving his farms and grounds that had suffered from his neglect during the war. Thanks to his overseer, Lund Washington, and to Washington's own input via letters of instruction, the estate had been maintained at a sufficient level to provide basic needs, but for increased productivity it needed his direct oversight. This is the task to which he now set his hand.

Not long after retiring to Mount Vernon, he wrote Maj. Gen. Henry Knox that it was taking some time to experience that ease and freedom from public cares. . . . I feel now, however, as I conceive a wearied Traveller must do, who, after treading many a painful step, with a heavy burden on his shoulders, is eased of the latter, having reached the Goal to which all the former were directed; and from his House top is looking back, and tracing with a grateful eye the Meanders by which he escaped the quicksands and Mires which lay in his way; and into which none but the All-powerful guide and great dispenser of human Events could have prevented his falling.[150]

It took some time for him to adjust to private life, but this was his goal as he wrote Lafayette in February 1784: "I am not only retired from all public employments, but I am retiring within myself; and shall be able to view the solitary walk, and tread the paths of private life with heartfelt satisfaction. Envious of none, I am determined to be pleased with all; and this my dear friend, being the order for my march, I will move gently down the stream of life, until I sleep with my Fathers."[151]

As the most famous man in the world, and with a nation struggling to be established in its newfound liberty, the stream of his life was not to be so serene and gentle. Friends and strangers flocked to Mount Vernon, where their high image of Washington was strengthened when he opened his home to them all. He and Martha showed great kindness and hospitality. He would also need the increased productivity of his estate to help pay for hosting the multitudes who came, many staying for a week or two.

While welcoming many guests, Washington still performed his daily duties. He would rise early in the morning for personal devotions,[152] reading, and writing until breakfast, which he enjoyed with his guests. After this, he would ride ten or twelve miles around the estate, attending to farm and business matters. Dinner was at three, where, according to G. W. P. Custis, "the general ate heartily, being no way particular, except as to fish, of which he was very fond."[153] He enjoyed conversing with his guests, which he would often do for two hours around dinner. The late afternoon he spent in his library with business correspondence or reading. In the evening he joined the family and guests for tea and more conversation, or if no guests were present, he often read aloud the newspaper or a good book. On Sundays he attended church, weather and roads permitting, and in the evening he would read aloud a sermon or a Christian book.[154]

Washington had simple habits throughout his life. He always rose early and was diligent in performing necessary and important tasks. He was very neat and always shaved himself quickly, so as to get on to the business awaiting him in the library. His breakfast was very simple, and his dinner table, while offering plenty to his guests, was not elaborate.

In September 1784, Washington made a 680-mile trip on horseback over the Allegheny Mountains, much of the trip being through the wilderness, to inspect lands he owned and to see if a passageway could be opened between the Potomac and James rivers, which flowed east, and other waters flowing west. He saw this as important in keeping the western settlers united with the new nation. He kept a detailed journal of his travels and discoveries and communicated this to the Virginia governor in October. Washington was the first to suggest to the new nation a number of internal improvements necessary to advance commerce in the west.

In his retirement years, he gave much time to his farming operations. As he had done prior to the war, he continued to plant wheat and other grains as his cash crop instead of tobacco, which depleted the soil. He instituted crop rotation, which proved very effective, and gave much time to planting trees and shrubs on the grounds of Mount Vernon. While greatly enjoying these agricultural and horticultural pursuits, much of his time was consumed with hosting a multitude of visitors and reading and responding to ever increasing correspondence. He wrote that these "deprive me of exercise, and unless I can obtain relief, must be productive of disagreeable consequences."[155] He finally had to hire a private secretary, Tobias Lear, to assist him.

In October 1785, in response to the state of Virginia resolving to erect a statue to honor Washington, the French artist Jean-Antoine Houdon spent three weeks at Mount Vernon, making exact molds of Washington to produce the most precise model that exists of the man. Houdon's statue now stands in the Virginia State capitol in Richmond. It was one of many statues and paintings that were executed of Washington during his lifetime.

During these retirement years, from 1783 to 1789, Washington made extensive improvements to his house, adding many rooms, the piazza on the riverfront, and the cupola on the roof, plus the kitchen and many other out-buildings, making it look much as it does today. These were probably the happiest days of his life, according to G. W. P. Custis.[156]

THE CONSTITUTIONAL CONVENTION

SINCE THE TIME OF the Revolutionary War, Washington had experienced the weaknesses of the national government under the Articles of Confederation. He wrote in March 1783, "No Man in the United States is, or can be more deeply impressed with the necessity of a reform in our present Confederation than myself. No Man perhaps has felt the bad effects of it more sensibly." He said the lack of congressional power prolonged the war and was the reason for most of his "perplexities," and "almost the whole of the difficulties and distress of the Army, have their origin here."[157]

Washington wrote in October 1785 that a central national power was needed to regulate commerce, arrange for the payment of war debts, and provide adequate national security.[158] The "thirteen sovereign independent, disunited States,"[159] which was what existed under the

Articles, could never operate properly to govern the new nation. A new national form of government was needed, but certainly not a monarchy, as some people were proposing. To follow this course would be a "triumph for the advocates of despotism" because it would show "we are incapable of governing ourselves, and that systems founded on the basis of equal liberty are merely ideal and fallacious!"[160] He added, "There are errors in our national government which call for correction; loudly."[161] Without a thorough reform, dissolution of the union of states would be inevitable.

A first step in what resulted in a new form of government occurred in 1785, when commissioners from five states met in Annapolis, Maryland, to discuss possible agreements regarding interstate trade, navigation, duties, and defense. But little was accomplished at this meeting because of the limited powers of the delegates and the number of states represented. The representatives, however, issued a report to all the states, pointing out the defects of the national government and the need to revise the Articles of Confederation. In addition, they recommended a convention should be held in May 1787 in Philadelphia with delegates from all the states, and that they be invested with sufficient power by their legislatures to resolve the crisis.

Virginia appointed seven delegates, with Washington at the head of the list. While he supported the goals of the convention, he did not believe it was proper for him to attend. In addition, he was "much afflicted with a Rheumatick complaint (of which I have not been entirely free for six months) as to be under the necessity of carrying my arm in a sling for the last ten days."[162] But many people impressed upon him the necessity of his participation for any hope of a successful outcome, and he agreed to go. Some friends, though, warned that if he did participate and the convention should fail to resolve the problem, his reputation would be greatly harmed. This argument, however, was no factor in his decision; Washington was as ready now as he had been during the war to risk his reputation, his property, and his life for a cause of such importance to his country and the advance of liberty.

Twelve states appointed the most prominent men of that day (or any age) to attend the convention, and all of them took great pains to prepare themselves for the task before them. John Adams studied the governments of fifty nations throughout history. Washington, whose experience already qualified him, reviewed the histories of numerous confederacies and wrote a paper analyzing how each had worked through their strengths and weaknesses.

Some delegates wanted only to revise the Articles of Confederation, which is what their state legislatures had empowered them to do, but Washington and others recognized much more was necessary. "My wish is," he wrote, "that the Convention may adopt no temporizing expedient, but probe the defects of the Constitution to the bottom, and provide radical cures."[163] Providentially, a radical cure was provided.

Washington was unanimously elected president of the convention, and he told the delegates that they may have a difficult time proposing a plan that would be adopted, but they must "raise a standard" of the best government they could conceive or else they may have to endure another war or worse. He declared, "The event is in the hands of God!"[164] As president, Washington did not enter into the debates, thus he could keep above the arguments. Yet he had great influence that summer by directing the proceedings and by informal discussions with the delegates when they were not in session.

The delegates agreed to form a new constitution. As the convention proceeded, little progress was made toward this goal because the delegates disagreed on many issues, especially regarding representation. By June 28, they were on the verge of collapse. At this point eighty-one-year-old Benjamin Franklin proposed that the delegates adjourn for three days to let their passions cool and take time to meet informally and discuss their opposite sentiments. Plus he called the convention to look to God for help. James Madison and other delegates recorded this famous appeal.

Franklin said they should humbly apply "to the Father of lights to illuminate our understandings," reminding the delegates that they had witnessed His providential favor throughout their struggle for independence. Addressing Washington, he continued,

> I have lived, Sir, a long time, and the longer I live, the more convincing proofs I see of this truth—that God governs in the affairs of man. And if a sparrow cannot fall to the ground without his notice, is it probable that an empire can rise without His aid? We have been assured, Sir, in the sacred writings that "except the Lord build the House they labour in vain that build it." I firmly believe this; and I also believe that without his concurring aid we

shall succeed in this political building no better, than the Builders of Babel.[165]

Franklin then suggested the convention obtain chaplains to open their daily sessions in prayer for God's assistance. Jonathan Dayton of New Jersey said that, after the doctor sat down, "never did I behold a countenance at once so dignified and delighted as was that of Washington, at the close of this address! Nor were the members of the Convention, generally less affected. The words of the venerable Franklin fell upon our ears with a weight and authority, even greater than we may suppose an oracle to have had in a Roman senate!"[166]

Franklin's proposal produced the desired result. After the recess, the atmosphere of the convention changed, and, Jonathan Dayton noted, "every unfriendly feeling had been expelled; and a spirit of conciliation had been cultivated,"[167] which enabled the delegates to reach a solution on the issue of representation as well as other matters. The compromises they reached, though not perfect, produced the best form of government ever devised by man. The U.S. Constitution has proven to be the most valuable civil document for the advancement of liberty in history.[168]

Washington wrote that he did not approve of everything in the Constitution, but "in the aggregate it is the best constitution, that can be obtained at this epoch."[169] The only other choice was dissolution of the union. Though the final document was not perfect, Washington observed, "It appears to me little short of a miracle" that the delegates, who represented such differences in manners and circumstances, "should unite in forming a system of national government, so little liable to well-founded objections."[170] He later wrote that the American system of government is "in my opinion the fairest prospect of happiness and prosperity that ever was presented to man."[171]

The Constitution was signed by all but three of the delegates present on September 17, 1787, and sent to the states for ratification. The debates of the various state conventions would be heated, and in many states, the votes close, but before the end of the summer of 1788, nine states had ratified the Constitution, which was enough for it to officially go into effect. Washington's name on the document provided much weight in the minds of the people as the states considered its approval.

Washington considered the formation and approbation of the Constitution a miracle. He wrote, "We may . . . trace the finger of Providence through those dark and mysterious events, which first induced the States to appoint a general Convention and then led them one after another . . . into an adoption of the system recommended by that general Convention." He believed the Constitution would most likely lay "a lasting foundation for tranquility and happiness," but knowing the source of blessing, his "earnest prayer" was "that the same good Providence may still continue to protect us and prevent us from dashing the cup of national felicity just as it has been lifted to our lips."[172]

By early 1789, twelve states had ratified the document and congressional elections were held. In March, electors from the states unanimously chose George Washington as the first president. Everyone knew he would be selected;

in fact, there may not have been anyone in the states who opposed this choice.[173] Other candidates would have faced opposition and potentially threatened the new union. Washington was the only man capable of unifying the American people at this critical time.

THE FIRST PRESIDENT

*O*N APRIL 16, two days after Washington was notified of his election as president, he set out from Mount Vernon to New York City, the home of the first constitutional government. He expressed his feelings in his diary entry: "About ten o'clock I bade adieu to Mount Vernon, to private life, and to domestic felicity; and, with a mind oppressed with more anxious and painful sensations than I have words to express, set out for New York . . . with the best disposition to render service to my country in obedience to its call, but with less hope of answering its expectations."[174]

He wrote to others of his great reluctance in assuming the duties bestowed upon him by his countrymen. He saw his inabilities to properly perform the task before him but vowed to do his best: "All I can promise is only to accomplish that which can be done by an honest zeal."[175] After expressing similar sentiments to the mayor and citizens of Alexandria, he wrote, "All that now remains for me is to commit myself and you to the protection of the beneficent Being, who, on a former occasion has happily brought us together, after a long and distressing separation. Perhaps the same gracious Providence will again indulge us with the same heartfelt felicity."[176]

Washington was greeted by large crowds and celebrations all along his route, none more elaborate and festive than when he arrived in New York on a splendidly outfitted barge to a thirteen-gun salute. Of his arrival in the city, Fisher Ames wrote, "When I saw Washington I felt very strong emotions. I believe that no man ever had so fair a claim to veneration as he."[177]

The day Washington took the oath of office, April 30, began with religious services in all the churches in the city. In the early afternoon, on the balcony at Federal Hall, he took the oath as prescribed by the Constitution, his hand on the Bible, added "so help me God,"[178] and then delivered his inaugural address, 40 percent of which was religious in nature. Following this, as resolved the day before by Congress, Washington and members of Congress went to St. Paul's Chapel "to hear divine service performed by the chaplains."[179]

In addition to townsfolk, farmers, and illustrious Americans, many foreigners and strangers gathered for the inauguration, "all anxious to witness the grand experiment that was to determine how much rational liberty mankind is capable of enjoying, without that liberty degenerating into licentiousness."[180]

His presidency began with an acknowledgment of God and appeal for His aid. Washington would need God's aid, for he was beginning a task where there were no examples in history for him to follow. He was overseeing the beginning and development of a new system of government, unlike any that had existed previously in the world. The destiny of his nation, as well as the future advancement of liberty, depended upon his every action.

Washington expressed in his inaugural address how he felt unqualified for the job, but he was prepared to respond to the call of duty from his country and fellow citizens. That alone was all that could motivate him to take on this difficult task. He was not seeking power, prestige, or pecuniary awards, for he declined all personal compensation, saying he would use his salary to cover his expenses. But his salary proved insufficient for even this, thus he drew upon his own funds to cover the difference.[181]

The first great task before Washington was the organization of the executive branch. The men he chose for his cabinet reveal his desire for the best-qualified people to fill the posts, rather than those who would always agree with him politically. He appointed Thomas Jefferson as head of the State Department, Alexander Hamilton to guide the Treasury, Henry Knox as secretary of war, and Edmund Randolph to be attorney general. In addition to carrying out Washington's directives in their respective spheres, these men provided advice and support in important matters. Washington solicited their views, weighed the arguments, and then made a decision, much as he had done with his councils of generals during the Revolutionary

War. On many issues the opinions of these men, especially Jefferson and Hamilton, were opposed.

Washington had to deal with a great number of applications for public office. He responded to each one in his own hand, which became "an almost insupportable burden to me."[182] His choices for government appointments reveal his wisdom and integrity, for these were made solely upon merit, not friendship nor for political rewards.

In addition to the challenges of his job, the hardships of life continued. In the summer of 1789, he became violently ill, almost to the point of death, and had to stay in bed for six weeks. It took twelve weeks to regain his strength, though he would never return to his previously robust stature. In August, his mother died at the age of eighty-two.

In October 1789, Washington took a monthlong tour of New England to meet with the citizens, observe their condition, and assess their feelings on the new government. Thousands of people turned out to greet him everywhere he went, not only in the cities and towns, but even assembling at crossroads where he was to pass. He received a hero's welcome, being seen by some almost as a god. This trip confirmed to Washington that the country was advancing and the future looked promising, in large part due to the integrity and industry of the American people.

Washington faced many major issues as president. Of great concern was the debt incurred during the war. Though not without great challenges, this issue was favorably resolved, as the federal government agreed to assume most of the national and state debts. Washington oversaw the design and building of the new national capital on the banks of the Potomac River. Though officially called the District of Columbia, it became known as Washington City, even in his lifetime. The construction of the capital occupied his time for a number of years.

The president's dealing with Indians was another important issue. His policy was to relate to the various tribes as he did any nation. He upheld treaties and acted toward them with kindness, justice, and humanity. When some tribes on the western frontiers initiated conflicts with settlers, he sent Gen. Anthony Wayne to wage war only as a last recourse, and it caused him much pain.

Though opposed by Jefferson and others, Washington approved the formation of a national bank. He believed it was the best means of dealing with the nation's debt and setting it on a sound financial footing.

In March 1791, Washington took a three-month tour of the southern states. His planning was so precise that he traveled 1,887 miles using the same horses and without an accident. He received the same admiration of the people and affirmation of the advancement of the nation as he had during earlier travels in the other states.

As the president's term of office was coming to a close much remained to be done to organize the country under the Constitution, to solidify the union, and to deal with the many challenges of the new nation. Early in 1792 many people appealed to Washington to seek a second term, seeing him as the only person to guide the new nation through the precarious events. Knowing of his desire to retire, three members of his cabinet, though representing different political views, wrote to the president and made the case for his reelection, asserting that he must serve another term for the good of the country, because only his character and steady hand could assure the country's preservation.

Jefferson said, "The confidence of the whole Union is centred in you. . . . North and south will hang together, if they have you to hang on." He pointed out how some men are chosen to sacrifice to lead mankind on the path of liberty: "This seems to be your condition, and the law imposed on you by Providence, in forming your character, and fashioning the events on which it was to operate. . . . I cannot but hope, that you can resolve to add one or two more to the many years you have already sacrificed to the good of mankind."[183]

Similarly, Hamilton strongly urged Washington: "The clear path to be pursued by you will be again to obey the voice of your country. I trust, and I pray God, that you will determine to make a further sacrifice of your tranquillity and happiness to the public good."[184] Edmund Randolph reminded Washington that "the constitution would never have been adopted, but from a knowledge that you had once sanctioned it, and an expectation that you would execute it." The nation still needed him, and Randolph appealed to his sense of duty. "It is the fixed opinion of the world, that you surrender nothing incomplete."[185]

Washington once again put the well-being of his nation above his own desires. He was unanimously reelected and took the oath of office on March 4, 1793.

The French Revolution had a major effect upon Washington's second term. In its initial stages, many in America saw the revolution as similar to their own: a struggle for the rights of all against the oppression of a ruling elite. However, as events unfolded, it became obvious that the foundational principles of the French Revolution were not the same as those of the American Revolution. The latter were rooted in a biblical worldview, but the former had their origins in humanism. The revolutionary French leaders saw man as the source of truth, virtue, and rights, and these were later centered in the government controlled by the revolutionaries. In contrast, America's Founding Fathers looked to God as the giver of life, liberty, and rights and to His Word, the Bible, as the source of truth.[186]

Before the fruit of bloodshed and chaos made clear the true nature of the French Revolution, many in America, including members of Washington's cabinet, urged the president to support France when the French declared war on England. After all, France had assisted America in her revolution and was seeking freedom itself. Washington's wisdom and resolve caused him to maintain a strict neutrality, which proved to be the best position the new nation could have taken. After soliciting the opinions of his cabinet in writing, Washington weighed their arguments and made a principled decision, issuing a proclamation of neutrality on April 22, 1793. Neutrality and impartiality, coupled with preparation for war in case it came, was, he believed, the best way to maintain peace with all nations. These ideas formed the foundation of American foreign policy and were emphasized in his Farewell Address a few years later.

Many people attacked Washington for this position, and the opposing views on support for the French contributed to the formation of two political parties: the Federalists and

Democratic-Republicans. But as a man of principle, Washington was not swayed by political pressure and the outcries of some agitated citizens. America maintained her neutrality throughout Washington's presidency.[187]

As his second term of office was coming to an end, many friends pressed him to serve again, but he had already determined his course of action. He made his retirement known formally in his Farewell Address, which was published on September 15, 1796, six months before his term expired. While not an official government document, the Farewell Address came to be considered, along with the Declaration and the Constitution, one of the three foundational components of American civil society. Washington's ideas of national unity, party spirit, foreign policy, and the religious foundation of civil society were not only prescient but also greatly influenced American thought and polity for more than a century.

In December, Washington gave his last speech to Congress. After presenting a clear picture of the condition of the country and his recommendations for continued advancement, he concluded: "I cannot omit the occasion to congratulate you and my country on the success of the experiment, nor to repeat my fervent supplications to the Supreme Ruler of the Universe and Sovereign Arbiter of Nations that His providential care may still be extended to the United States, that the virtue and happiness of the people may be preserved, and that the Government which they have instituted for the protection of their liberties may be perpetual."[188]

On March 4, 1797, George Washington was finally able to retire from civil service. He was glad to witness John

Adams take the oath of office in the hall of the House of Representatives in Philadelphia. In the celebrations that followed, Washington received more attention than the new president. As he returned home to Mount Vernon, he encountered well-wishers and exuberant demonstrations the entire way. He had more than performed his duty and left the nation on a solid foundation: credit had been restored, the public debt secured, commerce was increasing, the war with the Indians in the west had been successfully concluded, and peace had been maintained with the European nations. American liberty continued to advance, and the foundation of what would become the most free and prosperous nation in history was securely laid.

Final Retirement and Death

*W*ASHINGTON'S FINAL YEARS WERE summarized in a letter he wrote to a friend a few weeks after his return to Mount Vernon. As had always been his custom, he arose with the sun and prepared for the business of the day.

[B]y the time I have accomplished these matters, breakfast . . . is ready. This over, I mount my horse and ride round my farms, which employs me until it is time to dress for dinner; at which I rarely miss to see strange faces; come, as they say, out of respect to me. . . . [A]nd how different this, from having a few social friends at a cheerful board? The usual time of sitting at Table; a walk, and Tea, brings me within the dawn of Candlelight; previous to which, if not prevented by company, I resolve, that, as soon as the glimmering taper, supplies the place of

the great luminary, I will retire to my writing Table and
acknowledge the letters I have received; . . . having given
you the history of a day, it will serve for a year.[189]

A steady stream of visitors was about the only change
in this daily routine in the year that followed. Washington
was the most famous person in America and probably in
the world. As such, people from all over the country and
the globe wanted to meet him. He wrote his adopted son
in July 1797, "We have scarcely been alone a day for
more than a month, and now have a house full."[190] He
graciously received them all, not only entertaining them
at his table, but most would spend a number of nights at
Mount Vernon.

The routine of private life would be interrupted in the
summer of 1798, when Washington was once again
called upon to serve his country. French actions forced
Congress to authorize Adams to make preparations for
war, calling up a provisional army if war was declared
upon the United States. Adams asked Washington for his
help—"We must have your name"—and possibly his
presence as commanding general in the field.[191] Washington did not believe the French would invade America, but
he was ready to lead if necessary. "In case of actual Inva-
sion by a formidable force," he responded, "I certainly
should not Intrench myself under the cover of Age and retirement, if my services should be required by my Country, to assist in repelling it."[192] He was offered command of
the army, which he accepted on two conditions: first, that
he be able to appoint all principal officers, and second,
that he not physically go into the field unless war broke

out and the situation required it. As had been his prior example, he wanted no salary for his services.

While he never had to take the field, since war never occurred, he did devote much time during the remainder of his life to organizing the army, not only via much correspondence from Mount Vernon, but by spending a month in Philadelphia with Gens. Alexander Hamilton and Charles C. Pinckney, whom he had appointed. Washington believed the best way to maintain peace was to be always prepared for war. His convictions and sense of duty directed his public service until the end of his life. Washington did not live long enough to learn that Napoleon Bonaparte came to power in France and had no desire for war with the United States.

Washington was a strong, energetic, athletic man throughout his life. As was typical in his day, he suffered through a number of illnesses, at times laid up in bed for weeks. Yet when he retired from the presidency, he was in remarkably good health for a man in his midsixties. Thus on December 12, 1799, when he returned to Mount Vernon, wet and chilled from riding many hours around his farms in rain and sleet, he was not concerned when he came down with a sore throat. The next day a heavy snow kept him to only a short ride near his home. His sore throat worsened and he became hoarse, but still believed he only had a cold. He passed the evening in his usual cheerful conversation and reading, but before dawn of the next morning, December 14, he awoke with such soreness in his throat that he could barely talk or breathe.

Messengers were dispatched for three doctors, who arrived in the afternoon and tried their usual remedies for treating ague and a sore and swollen throat, including a number of bleedings, all with no positive effect. By evening, Washington was suffering greatly and only spoke with great difficulty and much pain. But he bore this with his characteristic resolve and lack of complaint. He was more concerned for others than himself, not wanting to be a burden to Martha or any of the doctors. He even motioned for one of his servants, who had been standing for a long time, to take a seat.

Washington's secretary, Tobias Lear, was present during the entire time, and he recorded the events in detail. As Washington weakened throughout the day, Lear lay upon the bed and assisted him when he changed positions. Washington expressed his gratitude and often said, "I am afraid I shall fatigue you too much." Lear said he gladly would do all he could to ease his pain, to which Washington replied, "Well, it is a debt we must pay to each other, and I hope, when you want aid of this kind, you will find it." During the day, George had given Martha instructions concerning his will and told Lear to remember to arrange his papers and settle his accounts in a proper manner. He also reminded them to bury his body in a decent manner at Mount Vernon in accordance with his previously stated wishes.[193]

Around five o'clock, Dr. James Craik entered the room. Washington said, "Doctor, I die hard, but I am not afraid to go. I believed, from my first attack, that I should not survive it. My breath cannot last long." Some years earlier, while president, Washington had expressed to his doctor, who was treating him for a violent illness, "I am not afraid to die. . . . Whether tonight, or twenty years hence, makes no difference; I know that I am in the hands of a good Providence."[194] His calm and peaceful manner as death approached affirmed his reliance on a good Providence.

He said a little later to those who were helping him, "I pray you to take no more trouble about me. Let me go off quietly. I cannot last long." Between ten and eleven o'clock, his breathing became easier, his pulse became weaker, and "he expired without a struggle or a sigh." When Martha, who was seated at the foot of the bed, finding solace in her Bible,[195] was told that he had passed, she said "'Tis well; all is now over; I shall soon follow him; I have no more trials to pass through."[196]

Washington faced death as he had lived his life: as a man of Christian character displaying resolve, peace, responsibility, and submission to the divine will. He was buried four days later on December 18 in the family tomb, just downhill from his beloved home, with the service performed by the Reverend Thomas Davis.[197]

Many years later, in the autumn of 1837, Washington's descendants, in accordance with his will, built a new vault farther down the hill and moved the remains there. The text of John 11:25 is inscribed over the vault door: "I am the resurrection, and the life: he that believeth in me, though he were dead, yet shall he live."[198]

The nation and the world mourned his death. His fame and hero status can be seen in the number of orations commemorating his life that were delivered in the year after his death. There were at least seven hundred sermons or general orations given in churches, colleges, schools, cities, and towns throughout America.[199] In many of these, Washington was likened to Moses, who led his people out of bondage, or Joshua, who led his people into the promised land, or the Savior, who delivered and gave birth to a new nation. Whether a commemorative sermon or a general oration, almost every one proclaimed that Washington had been raised up by Providence for the good of his people, the nation of America, and the advance of God's purposes in history.[200]

In a speech before the House of Representatives shortly after the death of Washington, John Marshall said, "Heaven has selected [Washington] as its instrument for dispensing good to man." He spoke of his unequaled contribution to liberty: "More than any other individual, and as much as to one individual was possible, has he contributed to found this our wide-spreading empire, and to give to the western world independence and freedom."[201]

The Senate wrote after hearing of his death that "his spirit is in Heaven" but "Washington yet lives on earth in his spotless example. . . . Let his countrymen . . . teach their children never to forget, that the fruits of his labors and his example are their inheritance."[202] It is vital for the cause of liberty that this inheritance be passed on to the American people today.

Part 2

The Character of George Washington

Washington is the mightiest name of earth—long since mightiest in the cause of civil liberty, still mightiest in moral reformation. On that name no eulogy is expected. It cannot be. To add brightness to the sun or glory to the name of Washington is alike impossible. Let none attempt it.

Abraham Lincoln

Principles of right conduct prevailed: there is no echo of any scandal, no hint of a breach of accepted morals, no line of obscenity, no reference to any sex experience, no slur on any woman.

In Washington this nation . . . has a man greater than the world ever knew, . . . a man dedicated, just and incorruptible, an example for long centuries of what character and diligence can achieve.

Douglas Southall Freeman

CHRISTIAN FAITH

*I shall rely, confidently, on that Providence which
has hitherto preserved and been bountiful to me.*

*T*HE GREATEST OF WASHINGTON'S character qualities was his strong Christian faith. This was
the key to his accomplishments and career. During his lifetime, and for many years after, almost no one would have
doubted that he was a Christian. Bishop William Meade
wrote, "Washington was regarded throughout America,
both among our military and political men, as a sincere
believer in Christianity, as then received among us, and a
devout man, is as clear as any fact in our history."[1]

In more recent years, some have made other claims. In
1989, the Mount Vernon Ladies' Association, the organization that maintains Mount Vernon, republished John Frederick Schroeder's 1854 *Maxims of Washington,* a
collection of Washington's words on a variety of subjects.
But while the quotes by Washington were basically the
same, the introductory remarks for each section were

changed. Under "Religious Maxims" in the republished version, Washington is called a deist.[2] In his original work, Schroeder gives quotations from contemporaries of Washington, like John Marshall, who said, "He was a sincere believer in the Christian faith."[3] Some historians today as well assert that Washington was not a Christian but a deist.[4] But the most prominent Washington biographers and compilers of his writings in the century and a half following his death[5] all said he was a Christian, as did his family, relatives, friends, and ministers.

Why the difference in views? It is not that more is known of his religious views today, but rather that those assessing his faith are mostly nonbelievers who have a secular view of history and therefore deliberately downplay faith or do not see faith as important in people's lives. If they are Christian, they offer a shallow assessment of Washington's faith or evaluate his faith in light of a modern perspective. Some, including some Christians, conclude he was a deist because, they say, he did not mention Jesus Christ, nor take communion, nor use modern evangelical language when writing about God, nor write a doctrinal position on what he believed. These items will be addressed later, but suffice it to say here that Washington did write of Jesus Christ, even calling Him divine. He also took communion at various times in his life. His writings are filled with acknowledgments of God and his belief in Him, and his language was similar to that of many orthodox ministers in the Episcopal Church, of which he was a member.[6]

Washington did not put forth in his writings a set of personal doctrines nor attempt to argue his particular

Christian dogma, since, as he said, he was not a preacher. Failure to do so does not exclude someone as a person of faith. Washington's faith reflected the Anglican/Episcopal tradition of which he was a part. His writings show he had a deep knowledge of the Bible, and his actions indicate he embraced the Christian faith. He was raised in a Christian home, attended church throughout his life, spent much time in private and public prayer, issued orders that promoted Christian living as essential, and had many testify he was a Christian. It rests upon those who claim he was not a Christian to prove so. Where is the proof that he was a deist? It cannot be seen in his writings or actions or testimonies of any who knew him.

There is no indication that he had a conversion experience, but this is the case of many raised in Christian homes. Washington may not have written of his heart's transformation, but his words and actions proclaim that he was Christian. In fact, many ministers and others have written that the fruit exemplified in Washington's life could have only been produced by the Christian faith.[7] He also encouraged others to embrace Christianity. The support for Washington's Christian faith is so great it would take a book to present it, and in fact a number of such books have been published.[8] The following is a brief overview of the evidence.

The words of his family and friends offer the strongest support of Washington's Christian faith, because they knew him most intimately. Chief Justice John Marshall was a close friend and was chosen by the family to write the president's biography; he asserted, "Without making ostentatious professions of religion, he was a sincere believer in the

Christian faith, and a truly devout man."[9] President of the Continental Congress during the Revolutionary War, Elias Boudinot, declared of Washington, "The General was a Christian."[10] Attorney Jonathan Mitchell Sewall added, "He was a firm believer in the Christian religion. . . . For my own part, I trust I shall never lose the impression made on my own mind in beholding—in this house of prayer—the venerable hero, the victorious leader of our hosts, bending in humble adoration to the God of armies and great Captain of our salvation!"[11]

Gunning Bedford Jr., a signer of the Constitution, said of his friend Washington: "To the character of hero and patriot, this good man added that of Christian. All his public communications breathe a pure spirit of piety, a resignation to the will of heaven and a firm reliance upon the providence of God. . . . Although the greatest man upon earth, he disdained not to humble himself before his God, and to trust in the mercies of Christ."[12]

Nelly Custis, Martha's granddaughter, was adopted by the Washingtons and lived at Mount Vernon for twenty years. In a letter to Jared Sparks, a chaplain of Congress and the first compiler of Washington's writings, she declared: "I should have thought it the greatest heresy to doubt his firm belief in Christianity. His life, his writings, prove that he was a Christian. . . . As well may we question his patriotism, his heroic, disinterested devotion to his country."[13]

Ministers who knew the president testified of his Christian faith as well. The Reverend Henry Muhlenberg, founder of the Lutheran Church in America, after visiting the general at Valley Forge, said: "George Washington . . .

respects God's Word, believes in the atonement through Christ, and bears himself in humility and gentleness."[14] The Reverend Devereux Jarratt pastored a church that Washington attended, and he noted, "He was a professor of Christianity and a member of the Protestant Episcopal Church."[15]

Family and friends affirmed his consistent devotional life as well. His nephew Robert Lewis spoke of his daily devotions,[16] and his adopted son, George Washington Parke Custis, said the general faithfully attended to the things of God in public and private life. The Reverend Lee Massey, Washington's pastor while he attended Pohick Church, said: "I never knew so constant an attendant on church as Washington. And his behaviour in the House of God, was ever so deeply reverential, that it produced the happiest effects on my congregation; and greatly assist me in my pulpit labours."[17]

As mentioned above, the early prominent biographers of Washington said he was a Christian. For example, Jared Sparks wrote of him, "A Christian in faith and practice, he was habitually devout."[18] Aaron Bancroft wrote, "In principle and practice he was a Christian."[19]

While president, Washington communicated with many different churches. His words to them show his great support for Christianity, and their words to him confirm his strong faith. The General Assembly of the Presbyterian Church in the U.S.A. sent a letter on May 26, 1789: "We . . . esteem it a peculiar happiness to behold in our Chief Magistrate, a steady, uniform, avowed friend of the Christian religion; who has commenced his administration in rational and exalted sentiments of piety; and who, in his private conduct, adorns the doctrines of the gospel of Christ; and on the most public and solemn occasions, devoutly acknowledges the government of Divine Providence."[20]

G. W. P. Custis said, "General Washington was always a strict and decorous observer of the Sabbath. He invariably attended divine service once a day, when within reach of a place of worship."[21] Many times, bad weather or roads kept Washington from traveling the great distance to his home churches—he attended Pohick Church before the war, which was about seven miles from Mount Vernon; after the war he attended Christ's Church in Alexandria, about ten miles away.[22] Nelly Custis wrote: "General Washington had a pew in Pohick Church, and one in Christ Church at Alexandria. He was very instrumental in establishing Pohick Church. . . . He attended the church at Alexandria, when the weather and roads permitted a ride of ten miles."[23]

Washington faithfully attended church and believed others should as well. In 1762, he rebuked his brother-in-law, Burwell Bassett, for not being at church and hearing the gospel, writing on August 28:

> Dear Sir: I was favoured with your Epistle wrote on a certain 25th of July when you ought to have been at Church, praying as becomes every good Christian Man who has as much to answer for as you have; strange it is that you will be so blind to truth that the enlightning sounds of the Gospel cannot reach your Ear, nor no Examples awaken you to a sense of Goodness; could you but behold with what religious zeal I hye me to Church

on every Lords day, it would do your heart good, and fill it I hope with equal fervency.[24]

Washington went to a variety of churches whenever he was away from home. When he was in Philadelphia in the fall of 1774 as a delegate to the First Continental Congress, he recorded attending "the Quaker meeting," "St. Peters," "to Christ Church," "to the Presbeterian Meeting," and "Romish Church."[25] While in the Boston area in 1775 and 1776, as commanding general, he found time to attend the Reverend Nathaniel Appleton's Congregational church as well as Christ Church (Episcopal). Throughout the war, he attended services in the various towns in which he had set up his headquarters. For example, the two winters he spent in Morristown, New Jersey, he attended the Presbyterian church pastored by Timothy Johnes.[26]

Nelly Custis commented that during his presidency, whenever Washington was "in New York and Philadelphia he never omitted attendance at church in the morning, unless detained by indisposition. . . . No one in church attended to the services with more reverential respect."[27] G. W. P. Custis wrote of his time with the Washingtons in Philadelphia: "On Sundays, unless the weather was uncommonly severe, the president and Mrs. Washington attended divine service at Christ Church; and in the evenings, the president read to Mrs. Washington, in her chamber, a sermon, or some portion from the sacred writings."[28] (He read sermons to his family when at home at Mount Vernon as well.[29]) When in New York, the Washingtons attended St. Paul's Church.

George Washington not only attended church regularly but for many years he served on the vestry of two different parishes, Fairfax and Truro, which included his two home churches, Pohick and Christ Church.[30] This was an elected position, so his fellow church members obviously considered him qualified to serve in this leadership role. His character was excellent, and his belief was orthodox. Capt. Azariah Dunham observed, "He had embraced the tenets of the Episcopal Church; yet his charity . . . led him equally to respect every denomination of the followers of Jesus."[31] There is no reason to believe from his words or actions that he held to anything but Protestant orthodoxy. He did not—like a deist—have a generic, all-inclusive set of tenets of faith. He certainly believed Roman Catholicism had errors; he wrote concerning Catholic Canadians that "a true Christian Spirit, will lead us to look with Compassion upon their Errors without insulting them."[32]

Washington's Christian faith is also evidenced by his many charitable contributions. Throughout his life, he generously gave to many churches, Bible societies, and gospel works. He had a heart for those in need and supported the poor in many ways (see pages 245–49, "Charity and Philanthropy").[33]

The writings of Washington reflect his intimate knowledge of God. He used at least eighty different names for "Jehovah, the Lord of Hosts," which shows great insight into the nature of the "Divine Author of Our Blessed Religion."[34] Washington often used biblical phrases in his writings, which reveal the depth of his knowledge of the Bible. In a "Circular to the States" (1782), he referred to Ecclesiastes 9:11 when he wrote "the race is not always to the swift, or the Battle to the strong."[35] Writing to the Marquis de Chastellux, he referred to Isaiah 2:4 in expressing his wish "that the swords might be turned into plough-shares, the spears into pruning hooks, and, as the Scripture expresses it, 'the nations learn war no more.'"[36] After that peace, he wrote to Lafayette, "I am become a private citizen on the banks of the Potomac, and under the shadow of my own Vine and my own Fig-tree . . . I am solacing myself,"[37] alluding to 1 Kings 4:25, Micah 4:4, and Zechariah 3:10. He liked the phrase "under my own Vine and fig tree" and used it often.[38] He spoke of Pharaoh in Exodus 5:7 who "compelled the Children of Israel to Manufacture Bricks without the necessary Ingredients."[39] He referred to "the widow's mite" (Mark 12:41–44; Luke 21:1–4) in a letter to his adopted son.[40] And there are many more biblical phrases in his writings.

His knowledge of God came from his parents, the church, and his personal studies. He had more than 150 sermons and Christian books in his library at his death.[41] One of the books in his library was a twenty-four-page handwritten manuscript entitled "The Daily Sacrifice." Some have suggested that this work, which contains daily prayers with very explicit Christian content, was written by Washington when he was a young man, though there is no direct evidence of this.[42] Since he knew the importance of a Christian education, he gave Bibles and prayer books to Martha's children and sent his grandson and adopted son to be taught by ministers at Princeton and St. John's colleges.

Washington prayed, read the Bible, and had personal devotions throughout his life. His nephew, Robert Lewis, was his private secretary during the first part of his presidency and lived with Washington for a time. Lewis noted, "He had accidentally witnessed his private devotions in his library both morning and evening; that on those occasions he had seen him in a kneeling posture with a Bible open before him, and that he believed such to have been his daily practice."[43]

While Washington was generally reserved in expressing his faith, he did not neglect public prayers. He prayed for his family and his nation. Just prior to his stepdaughter Martha Parke Custis's sudden death at Mount Vernon, Washington "knelt by her and prayed most fervently, most affectingly, for her recovery," according to Nelly Custis, the niece of Patsy and daughter of Martha.[44] He concluded his 1783 "Circular to the Governors of the States," with a prayer: "I now make it my earnest prayer, that God would have you and the State over which you preside, in his Holy protection."[45]

He prayed at meals regularly. The artist James Sharples, who spent time at Mount Vernon painting Washington's portrait, said: "I observed that we never partook of food without the general offering grace to the Giver, so also at the close of every repast."[46] He participated in special days of prayer. On June 1, 1774, Virginia observed a day of fasting, humiliation, and prayer to show support for the people of Boston. In his diary, Washington recorded: "Went to Church & fasted all day."[47] He observed similar days proclaimed by Congress throughout the Revolutionary War.

Washington respected and entertained many clergymen and was also close with some, including the Reverends Lee Massey, William White, and John Carroll.[48] Ministers and church bodies respected him greatly. Maj. William Jackson, aide-de-camp to Washington, said he was "beloved and admired by the holy ministers of religion."[49]

Washington believed in the afterlife[50] and was not afraid to die. When faced with a severe illness while president, he told his doctor, "I am not afraid to die, . . . I know that I am in the hands of a good Providence."[51] About ten years later he faced death calmly, saying, "I am ready to go." His last will and testament begins, "In the name of God, Amen."[52]

Although Washington was reserved in expressing his faith, one would not know it from his public actions. He carried on his personal devotional life wherever he was, whether at home at Mount Vernon, as president, or in his field tent. During the French and Indian War, an aide, Col. B. Temple, testified "that on sudden and unexpected visits into his [Washington's] marquee, he has, more than once, found him on his knees at his devotions."[53] It was said of Washington, in a sketch written by an American in London in 1779 that "he regularly attends divine service in his tent every morning and evening, and seems very fervent in his prayers."[54]

Washington also regularly prayed in public. He said grace at public meals where no chaplain was present. An attendant at a state dinner in May 1789 noted, "As there was no chaplain present, the President himself said a very short grace as he was sitting down."[55] The chaplain of Congress would dine with him once a month during Washington's presidency. Washington would ask him to pray at these meals. At one such meal, likely forgetting that Chaplain Ashbel Green was present, the president began to ask a blessing, but after a few words, he bowed to Green and asked him to proceed, which Green noted, "I accordingly did. I mention this because it shows that President Washington always asked a blessing himself, when a chaplain was not present."[56] Green added that Washington "always, unless a clergyman was present at his own table, asked a blessing, in a standing posture. If a clergyman were present, he was requested both to ask a blessing and to return thanks after dinner."[57]

Numerous days of prayer were proclaimed by various governmental bodies during Washington's lifetime. His habit was to observe these days diligently, at times attending public church services and at times participating with his troops in the field. In 1774, he observed such a day by fasting.[58] He observed many days of prayer during the Revolutionary War. He and Martha attended services at the Princeton College chapel on October 31, 1783, in celebration of the signing of the peace treaty that ended the war. In response to the recommendation of Congress for Americans to observe thanksgiving services to mark the end of the war, the Washingtons attended church in Philadelphia on December 11, 1783.[59]

Many prayers for people, leaders, and the nation can be found in his public writings. This was especially true throughout the war. On July 4, 1775, just after assuming command of the Continental army in Massachusetts, he ended his response to an address by the Massachusetts legislature "earnestly implor[ing] the divine Being, in whose hands are all human events," to bring private and public happiness to them.[60] In his farewell orders to the army on November 2, 1783, he offered "his prayers to the God of Armies" that "ample justice be done them here, and may the choicest of heaven's favours, both here and hereafter, attend those who, under the devine auspices, have secured innumerable blessings for others."[61]

During both of his administrations, he issued proclamations and observed them. According to the chaplain of the House of Representatives, Ashbel Green, "the proclamations which he issued for the purpose were probably written by himself,"[62] in contrast to John Adams, who had the chaplains write his proclamations. In October 1789, Washington issued a proclamation for a day of prayer and thanksgiving to be observed on November 26 with the opening words: "Whereas it is the duty of all nations to acknowledge the providence of Almighty God, to obey His will, to be grateful for His benefits, and humbly to implore His protection and favor."[63] Washington sought to do this throughout his life, and he also believed the Christian nation of America should do so too. But even more than this, he believed that all nations should acknowledge God's providence and obey His will.

Washington knew how morality and religion were linked to success in military endeavors, and so he issued orders to procure chaplains for the army during the Revolutionary War. He directed his field commanders: "to procure Chaplains . . . ; persons of good character and exemplary lives; to see that all inferior officers and soldiers . . . attend carefully upon religious exercises. The blessing and protection of Heaven are at all times necessary, but especially so in times of publick distress and danger. The General hopes and trusts that every officer and man will endeavor so to live and act as becomes a Christian soldier defending the dearest rights and liberties of his country."[64]

Washington encouraged his troops to seek God and to live like Christians. He ordered them to attend worship services and to observe days of prayer and thanksgiving. A few days after Washington took command of the army in Massachusetts, the Reverend William Emerson, an army chaplain, wrote that each day's orders were read to the regiments "every morning after prayers."[65] On March 6, 1776, Washington ordered the troops to observe a day of fasting, prayer, and humiliation, as directed by the state legislature,[66] and he reminded the soldiers at Valley Forge, "To the distinguished character of a Patriot, it should be our highest glory to add the more distinguished character of a Christian."[67] He issued orders against "profane cursing and swearing," saying that "we can have little hopes of the blessings of Heaven on our Arms, if we insult it by our impiety, and folly; added to this, it is a vice so mean and low, without any temptation, that every man of sense, and character, detests and despises it."[68] The general also issued orders prohibiting gambling[69] and drunkenness.[70]

As already mentioned, Washington observed the Sabbath throughout his life. He encouraged his troops to do so as well by having the chaplains perform regular Sunday services and not scheduling exercises on

Sundays if possible. His general orders of March 22, 1783, state:

> In justice to the zeal and ability of the Chaplains, as well as to his own feelings, the Commander in chief thinks it a duty to declare the regularity and decorum with which divine service is now performed every Sunday, will reflect great credit on the army in general, tend to improve the morals, and at the same time, to increase the happiness of the soldiery, and must afford the most pure and rational entertainment for every serious and well disposed mind.
>
> No fatigue except on extra occasions, nor general review or inspections to be permitted on the Sabbath day.[71]

If no chaplains were present, Washington would, at times, conduct services himself. When Edward Braddock was buried after the battle of the Monongahela in 1755, "Washington read the impressive funeral services of the Anglican church, over his body."[72] In the years that followed, one of Washington's aides, Col. B. Temple, observed, "Frequently on the Sabbath, he has known Colonel Washington to perform divine service with his regiment, reading the scriptures and praying with them, when no chaplain could be had."[73]

Washington administered the oath of allegiance to his officers in the customary manner, with them standing around him in a circle and together taking hold of a Bible.[74] He himself took the oath of office as president with his hand on the Bible.[75] Washington also supported the dissemination of Bibles among the troops.[76]

Washington's public writings and letters provide massive evidence in support of his Christian faith, character, and worldview. Throughout his life, and especially during the war, he acknowledged the hand of God and Providence, writing of needing His aid and recognizing that success depended upon Him. His most significant and widely read writings all reflect a strong declaration of his Christian faith and worldview. This includes his "Circular to the Governors of the States" (June 8, 1783[77]; see pages 165–73, "Christian Character and Morality"), his first inaugural address (April 30, 1789),[78] and his Farewell Address (1796).[79]

There was great mutual respect between Washington and the clergy. The president's adopted son wrote: "The high respect in which the clergy of the American army was held by Washington was known to every officer and soldier in its ranks."[80] After Washington was elected president, many churches and denominations wrote him letters of congratulations and support.[81] This correspondence shows his Christian faith. The letters thank him for his support of Christian liberty and the Christian faith. His replies, according to Sparks, "breathe a Christian spirit" and imply his belief "of the truth and authority of the Christian religion."[82]

Washington supported Christianizing the Indians for their benefit as well as the nation's. In 1779, he wrote to the chiefs of the Delawares: "You do well to wish to learn our arts and ways of life, and above all, the religion of Jesus Christ. These will make you a greater and happier people than you are."[83] As president, he wrote to the United Brethren for Propagating the Gospel among the Heathen, saying that it would be a good thing for the government to cooperate with the "endeavors of your Society to civilize and Christianize the savages of the wilderness."[84]

In summary, Washington was a devoted churchgoer but not a sectarian. He did not write about his doctrinal beliefs, but his life and writings reflect orthodoxy. He regularly prayed in public and private, but he never spoke of his private devotions. His adopted daughter wrote, "He was not one of those who act or pray, 'that they may be seen of men.' He communed with his God in secret."[85] Since he did not speak about himself on any personal matter, it follows that he would not speak of his religious beliefs.

Jared Sparks commented, "To say that he was not a Christian, or at least that he did not believe himself to be a Christian, would be to impeach his sincerity and honesty."[86] After studying his life and writings extensively, Sparks added, "I have never seen a single hint, or expression, from which it could be inferred, that he had any doubt of the Christian revelation."[87]

Those who assert that Washington was a deist argue that he did not write of Jesus Christ but used vague, general terms, thus he could not be a Christian. Yet, as mentioned above, he wrote to the Delaware chiefs that they should learn "the religion of Jesus Christ."[88] He also wrote of "the Divine Author of our blessed Religion," clearly speaking of Jesus, and calling Him "Divine." Many of the eighty terms he used for God in his writings express the nature of the Christian deity and His Son, not a deistic view of God.[89] These also show he had a great knowledge of the nature of God.

Some also argue that Washington used deistic terminology, not Christian; for example, referring to Providence as "it." As stated above, Washington used Christian language throughout his life, including many biblical phrases. Much of his terminology was like that which was used by devout Episcopalians of the time, including their ministers.[90] Washington did use "it" at times for Providence, but since Providence is "the superintending care of God over His creation,"[91] then "it" is an appropriate way to reference this. Also, he used "He" many times when referring to the "Almighty Being,"[92] "benign Parent," and so on. Jonathan Mitchell Sewall observed: "Let the deist reflect on this, and remember that Washington, the saviour of his country, did not disdain to acknowledge and adore a greater Saviour, whom deists and infidels affect to slight and despise."[93]

Another argument used to expound on Washington's supposed deism is the assertion that he did not take communion. While this appears to be true for part of his time as president (and the reason had nothing to do with a lack of Christian belief, because, among many other things, he continued to faithfully attend church),[94] he took communion many times, and many people have attested of this, including his granddaughter, Nelly Custis. She wrote that she heard her mother say, "General Washington always received the sacrament with my grandmother before the Revolution."[95]

If Washington was a deist, then we would expect some ministers of his day to point out this fact or express some doubts of his Christianity. They challenged the faith of other prominent founders (Benjamin Franklin, Thomas Paine, and Thomas Jefferson), but not Washington.[96]

The arguments put forth by those claiming Washington was a deist are weak. His life, words, character, and action proclaim what his family and friends witnessed to: he was a sincere Christian believer.

MASONIC ACTIVITY

Of my Presiding over the English Lodges in this country. The fact is, I preside over none, nor have I been in one more than once or twice, within the last thirty years.

*J*ESUS SAID THAT WE would know the faith of men by their fruit—fruit revealed in personal character and outward action. In both, Washington demonstrated that he was a solid Christian. But when one speaks of Washington's Christian character, some object, pointing out that he owned slaves and was a Freemason, and thus could not be considered a good Christian or, at the least, he had grave shortcomings regarding these matters. These two issues will be addressed before examining Washington's many Christian qualities.

Was Washington a Mason? And if he was, how could he reconcile this with his Christian faith? In brief, Washington did join the Freemasons, but he was not very active, especially in his later years. Even so, Freemasonry in early America was much different than it is today. It was a kind of Christian social club. This is why Washington and a few founders joined the organization.[97]

Washington's writings reveal his minimal involvement in the Masons, and leading Masonic historians confirm this. William Adrian Brown, former librarian at the George Washington Masonic Memorial in Alexandria, Virginia, records twenty-nine links or encounters between Washington and Masonry throughout the president's life, and most of these were superficial and not initiated by Washington. These include gifts that were sent to Washington by Freemasons, greetings extended to him by groups of Masons, and letters from Masonic groups.

The list of twenty-nine encounters includes public events at which Washington was present and some Masons were also in the crowd, such as Washington's inaugurations and public parades. This list includes events that Washington did not attend, such as four meetings at certain lodges where Washington was proposed as grand master, which he declined, or where he was nominated as an honorary member. The significant contacts that he initiated were few. He joined the Masons on November 4, 1752, at the age of twenty. During the next year he went to two other meetings. He took the three steps of Freemasonry, but no higher degrees, for such was not integrated into American Freemasonry until well after Washington's death. By 1755 he had attended two more meetings. His next Masonic activity, according to Brown, did not occur until twenty-three years later: a parade on December 28, 1778, where Washington and the participants marched to Christ Church in Philadelphia to attend services. There were six other similar events during the Revolutionary

War. After the war, he attended one lodge meeting on June 24, 1784, and a funeral of a fellow Mason in 1785. His last Masonic encounter was the laying of the cornerstone of the Capitol in 1793.[98]

Of Brown's list of encounters, fourteen at most were genuinely Masonic, and most of these were when Washington was young. Thus Washington was not an active Mason.

It is important also to realize that Freemasonry in the mid- and late-1700s was much different than today. The non-Christian aspects of Freemasonry today did not exist in the Freemasonry of Washington's day. The Scottish Rite with its thirty-two degrees and its secret and non-Christian nature was not created until after Washington's death. The Founding Fathers who became Masons saw the group as a service organization. William Wirt, U.S. attorney general, joined the Masons as a young man, but he became a crusader against Masonry when it began to change in later years. He wrote: "I . . . continually regarded Masonry as nothing more than a social and charitable club, designed for the promotion of good feeling, among its members and for the pecuniary relief of their indigent brethren." But he then spoke against what Masonry had become, considering "it at war with the fundamental principles of the social compact, as treason against society, and a wicked conspiracy against the laws of God and man, which ought to be put down."[99]

Not only was early Freemasonry largely a social club, it actually embraced orthodox Christianity. An early Masonic guide (first printed in 1756) set forth a model prayer for use in American lodges: "Most holy and glorious Lord God . . . in Thy name we assemble and meet together, most humbly beseeching Thee to bless us in all our undertakings, that we may know and serve Thee aright, that all our doings may tend to Thy glory and the salvation of our souls. . . . This we most humbly beg, in the name and for the sake of Jesus Christ, our Lord and Savior. Amen."[100]

In 1749, Charles Brockwell reminded a Masonic lodge: "Whoever is an upright Mason can neither be an atheist, deist, or libertine; for he is under the strictest obligation to be . . . a true Christian."[101] Wellins Calcott wrote in 1769 that a "good Mason is a good man, and a good Christian."[102] And William Hutchinson stated in 1775 in the *Spirit of Freemasonry*: "The Master Mason represents a man under the Christian doctrine, saved from the grave of iniquity and raised to the faith of salvation. As the great testimonial that we are risen from the state of corruption, we bear the emblem of the Holy Trinity as the insignia of our vows."[103]

Even in 1818, less than ten years before Freemasonry began to change, the Christian nature of the membership was still evident. A Masonic work published that year stated: "Masonic faith acknowledges the Holy Bible to be the Word of God—that it was written by persons divinely inspired and reveals the whole duty of man. . . . [A]bove all, it is not, neither can it be a secret, that a good Mason is of necessity, truly and emphatically, a Christian."[104]

Many sermons were preached at Masonic meetings that show that Christianity was embraced by early Masonry in America. The Reverend William Smith preached to the Freemasons of Pennsylvania in 1778: "When our master, Christ, shall come again to reward his faithful workmen and servants . . . let us remember that it will be assuredly asked—were we of Christ Jesus?"[105] In fact, the services in early Masonic meetings were only conducted by Christian ministers, who preached gospel messages. In addition, many orthodox Christian clergy were Freemasons, seeing no discrepancy between the two.[106] There were no blood oaths in early Masonry in America as there are today.[107]

To summarize, in the words of Robert Morey, a historian of Freemasonry in America, it is "crystal clear that Freemasonry was understood to be a Christian institution until the anti-Masonic movement of 1826."[108]

Many Masons today, with many Christians accepting their claims (even writing books lamenting the fact), state that the vast majority of the Founders were Freemasons and attribute great influence to the Masons in the establishment of America. The majority of Founders, however, were not Masons, and their influence has been greatly overstated. Even though early Masonry was not incompatible with Christianity, most of the Founders were not Masons. In fact, less than 20 percent of the Founders were Masons. Modern Masons have tried to exploit the Founders to benefit their cause. In Washington's case, this was done during his lifetime.

As has been stated, Washington joined the Masons in his youth, but he was not active. As his fame grew, various Masonic lodges attempted to draw upon his popularity and seek his support. Some lodges made him an honorary member; at other lodge meetings, Washington was proposed as the general grand master of the United States (only proposed), and the Alexandria lodge named him their charter master. He was not present at any of these meetings nor gave his consent to the nominations.[109] These honorary titles and proposals were communicated to the public in such a way that at least one minister believed Washington was the acting grand mason over all the English lodges in America.

In 1798, the Reverend G. W. Snyder sent Washington a copy of *Proofs of a Conspiracy* that offered an account of the "Society of Illuminati" and its attempt to execute a plan to "overturn all Government and all Religion" by propagating their tenets through Masonic lodges.[110] Snyder added, "I was led to think, that it might be within your power to prevent the horrid plan from corrupting the brethren of the lodges over which you preside."[111]

In reply, Washington wrote on September 25, 1798:

> I have heard much of the nefarious, and dangerous plan, and doctrines of the Illuminati, but never saw the Book until you were pleased to send it to me. . . . [T]hanks for your kind wishes and favorable sentiments, except to cor rect an error you have run into, of my Presiding over the English Lodges in this country. The fact is, I preside over none, nor have I been in one more than once or twice, within the last thirty years. I believe notwithstanding, that none of the Lodges in this Country are contaminated with the principles ascribed to the Society of the Illuminati.[112]

On October 24, Washington wrote a second letter to Snyder and clarified his view that, while he believed some of the doctrines of the Illuminati had spread into the United States, he did not believe the Masonic lodges in America had been influenced by these ideas.[113]

Since Washington's death, the Masons have tried to exploit him with spurious images of him in Masonic garb and by building a Masonic memorial to him, giving the impression he was a devoted Mason. In reality, he participated in Masonic activities no more than a dozen times in his life.

In summary, Washington had minimal involvement with Masonry. He saw the Masons as a service organization, and in his day, Masonry was compatible with Christianity. The more ungodly elements in Masonry came in after Washington's time. The Masons exploited the fame of Washington for their benefit.

Washington and Slavery

There is not a man living, who wishes more sincerely than I do, to see a plan adopted, for the abolition of it [slavery].

*W*HILE WASHINGTON OWNED SLAVES, he was an early pioneer to end slavery in Virginia and the United States. He was against slavery and signed the first federal antislavery legislation in 1789: the Northwest Ordinance prohibited slavery in the northwest (present-day Indiana, Illinois, Michigan, Minnesota, Ohio, and Wisconsin). Washington wrote in 1786: "I can only say that there is not a man living who wishes more sincerely than I do, to see a plan adopted for the abolition of it [slavery]."[114]

Washington's view of slavery was in line with a majority of the Founding Fathers'. They believed slavery was fundamentally wrong and should be abolished, that blacks had the same God-given inalienable rights as all people.[115] They not only believed this, they also acted on it. Many of the Founders initiated antislavery societies. After securing the country's independence, many worked to end slavery in the states (some antislavery actions before independence were thwarted by the British government)[116]—one half of the states abolished slavery within a few decades of independence. Less than 50 percent of the signers of the Declaration and the Constitution owned slaves, and many who did emancipated them. More than 70 percent were antislavery. Washington was one who had slaves and was antislavery.

Washington became a slave owner at age eleven, when his father died and he inherited slaves. He would inherit others later from other family members. He was surrounded by slavery, but he nonetheless developed a conviction that slavery was wrong and should be abolished. It should be remembered that the Founders inherited slavery in America; they did not create it. They took great steps to end this evil institution. While more could have been done, they probably did more to eliminate slavery than any other group of leaders up until that time in history.

Even though Washington owned slaves, he wanted the states to end the evil practice. Before independence, he expressed his opinion in the Fairfax County resolutions of July 18, 1774 (he chaired the committee):[117] "No slaves ought to be imported into any of the British Colonies on this Continent; and we take this opportunity of declaring our most earnest wishes to see an entire stop forever put to such a wicked, cruel, and unnatural trade."[118] He later wrote to nephew Lawrence Lewis, "I wish from my soul that the Legislature of this State could see the policy of a gradual Abolition of Slavery."[119] He worked throughout his life to get Virginia to end the slave trade, to abolish slavery, and to change the laws to allow slave owners to free their slaves. But he had only limited success. Laws were passed to end the slave trade, but Virginia's laws were not modified to allow easy freedom for slaves. Nevertheless, he found a way to get around the laws as he made a provision in his will to free his slaves.

While he and other prominent Founding Fathers from Virginia (such as Jefferson, George Mason, and Henry Lee) worked to end slavery in their state, many in the state legislature were not convinced. Since Virginia law did not allow him to emancipate his slaves, the only legal means at his disposal to alter the status of his slaves was to sell them, a practice he opposed. He explained: "Were it not that I am principled against selling Negroes . . . I would not in twelve months from this date be possessed of one as a slave."[120]

Washington bought some fifty slaves before the Revolution, though he purchased none afterward; by then he had decided to no longer participate in the slave trade nor buy or sell slaves. He wrote: "I never mean . . . to possess another slave by purchase; it being among my first wishes to see some plan adopted, by which slavery in this country may be abolished by slow, sure, and imperceptible degrees."[121]

Washington demonstrated his firm conviction against slavery in many ways. He worked to change the state laws, he signed federal legislation as president, and he refused to sell slaves even though it was a financial hardship to keep them. He had many more slaves than were financially profitable—he wrote, "A full half than can be employed to any advantage in the farming system." While he would have reaped great economic benefits, he refused to sell any slaves: "To sell the overplus I cannot, because I am principled against this kind of traffic in the human species. To hire them out is almost as bad because they could not be disposed of in families to any advantage, and to disperse [break up] the families I have an aversion."[122]

He not only refused to sell slaves, he refused to break up families. He also felt responsible for taking care of his slaves until there was a "plan adopted by which slavery in this country may be abolished." A general plan did not materialize in Virginia (as it did in many other states), but Washington found a loophole that allowed him to get around the state law: emancipating his slaves at his death. His last will and testament not only gave his slaves their freedom but also made provision for them as they began to live as free citizens.[123]

Washington suffered no racial bigotry. He allowed free blacks to enlist in the army, thus creating the first interracial army in America; this did not occur again until the 1950–53 Korean War.[124] He approved Benjamin Banneker, a free black, as a surveyor to lay out Washington, D.C. He supported Phillis Wheatley, a black poet. There are numerous examples of his respect for many blacks, who in return respected him greatly. Some of his former slaves voluntarily maintained his tomb for decades after his death.

CHRISTIAN CHARACTER AND MORALITY

A good moral character is the first essential in a man. It is therefore highly important, to endeavor not only to be learned, but virtuous.

*W*ASHINGTON BELIEVED THAT NO nation could long endure without a virtuous and moral people. A loss of principles and manners was the greatest threat to a free people and would cause a nation's downfall more surely than any foreign enemy. In his 1796 Farewell Address, Washington wrote: "Of all the dispositions and habits which lead to political prosperity, religion and morality are indispensable supports."[125] He wrote in 1797: "Religion and Morality are the essential pillars of Civil society."[126]

Washington not only spoke of the societal value of morality and Christian character, but he displayed it. He was a great example in word and deed. As he was disbanding the Continental army, he wrote a letter to the governors of all the states on June 8, 1783, giving his advice on what needed to be done to assure the success of the newly formed nation: "I now make it my earnest prayer, that God would have you, and the State over which you preside, in his holy protection . . . that he would most graciously be pleased to dispose us all to do justice, to love mercy, and to demean ourselves with that charity, humility, and pacific temper of mind, which were the characteristics of the Divine Author of our blessed religion, and without an humble imitation of whose example in these things, we can never hope to be a happy nation."[127] His advice to the governors was to imitate Jesus Christ and His character.

Washington himself reflected the divine Author of his blessed religion in many ways. One example is seen in his response to the attempt to make him king. After the fighting had ceased and negotiations were beginning to officially end the war, many people were looking for a way to deal with the problems the new nation faced. Since many of Washington's officers had not received their promised pay, they were especially aware of Congress's weaknesses in handling the difficulties of governing the nation. Several officers proposed making Washington king as the best means of averting national collapse. The people loved him, and the officers would support him, and both knew he would act benevolently. Col. Lewis Nicola presented this idea to Washington in a letter in the spring of 1782. Washington's reply reveals his character:

> Sir, With a mixture of great surprise and astonishment I have read with attention the Sentiments you have submitted to my perusal. Be assured Sir, no occurrence in the course of the War, has given me more painful sensations

than your information of there being such ideas existing in the Army as you have expressed, and I must view with abhorrence, and reprehend with severity. . . .

I am much at loss to conceive what part of my conduct could have given encouragement to an address which to me seems big with greatest mischiefs that can befall my Country. If I am not deceived in the knowledge of myself, you could not have found a person to whom your schemes are more disagreeable.[128]

After strongly rebuking Nicola (who wrote three letters of apology afterward[129]), Washington examined his own heart to ensure that he had done nothing to communicate any such desire within him. His strength of character helped to assure the survival and success of the new nation. Both leaders and citizens must practice "morality" and "religious obligations" which, according to Washington, are "a necessary spring of popular government" and "the strongest claims to national and individual happiness."[130]

Washington's morality and numerous facets of his character were never more clearly displayed than during the winter at Valley Forge. Few men, if any, could have led the army through this time, called "the crucible of freedom."[131]

The winter of 1777/78 was one of the most important in our nation's history, for that winter, when the Continental army faced as great an ordeal as any army in history, was the turning point of the American Revolution. Prior to its movement to Valley Forge in December 1777, Washington's army was an undisciplined mob with few victories to show for their efforts; however, the next spring those same men marched out of camp as a disciplined band committed to their general and the cause of liberty and prepared for victory.

What was the ordeal this army faced? How did such a change occur during the months at Valley Forge? What was the cause behind this change?

When the army entered Valley Forge, the troops lacked clothes, tents, and blankets. Washington wrote that being "without shoes," their "marching through frost and snow . . . might be traced by the blood from their feet, and almost as often without provisions as with."[132] And their situation only worsened after December 19. Washington pleaded for supplies for his men from Congress. In a December 23, 1777, letter to Congress, Washington wrote that a number of men were confined to hospitals and in farmers' homes "for want of shoes. . . . [W]e have, by a field return this day made no less than 2898 Men in Camp unfit for duty because they are barefoot and otherwise naked."[133]

About one-third of all his troops were unfit for service, and this number only increased as winter progressed. "The unfortunate soldiers were in want of everything. They had neither coats, hats, shirts, nor shoes," wrote Lafayette. "The men," said Friedrich von Steuben, "were literally naked, some of them in the fullest extent of the word."[134]

Hunger was an even greater danger. "The army frequently remained whole days without provisions," said Lafayette. "One soldier's meal on a Thanksgiving Day declared by Congress was a 'half a gill of rice and a tablespoonful of vinegar!' In mid-February there was more than a week when the men received no provisions at all."[135] Dr. Albigence Waldo gave this description: "There comes a soldier, his bare feet are seen through his worn out shoes, his legs nearly naked from the tattered remains of an only pair of stockings; his breeches are not sufficient to cover his nakedness, his shirt hanging in strings, his hair dishevelled, his face meagre. His whole appearance pictures a person forsaken and discouraged. He comes and cries with an air of wretchedness and despair, 'I am sick, my feet lame, my legs are sore, my body covered with this tormenting itch.'"[136]

Due to this lack of food and clothing, hundreds of Washington's troops fell sick. Many men's "feet and legs froze till they became black, and it was often necessary to amputate them."[137] During most of January and February there were "constantly more than 4,000 soldiers who were incapacitated as a result of exposure, disease, and undernourishment."[138]

And in the midst of all of this, they persevered! Beyond this, the patient attitude with which they endured this misery was no less than supernatural. On April 21, 1778, Washington wrote to a congressional delegate: "For without arrogance, or the smallest deviation from the truth it may be said, that no history, now extant, can furnish an instance of an Army's suffering such uncommon hardships as ours has done, and bearing them with the same patience and Fortitude. . . . [Their] submitting without a murmur, is a mark of patience and obedience which in my opinion can scarce be parallel'd."[139]

What could possibly have held this army together through this ordeal? Friedrich von Steuben observed that no European army could have held together under such circumstances. How, then, could an inexperienced army stick together? Was it due to good discipline? "With regard to military discipline," von Steuben stated, "no such thing existed."[140]

Could it have been the financial reward they would receive? Their paltry pay was already four to five months past due, and complete payment would never come for many of them. Most historians agree that the army persevered at Valley Forge because of the troops' love of liberty and their devotion to Washington. George Bancroft commented that "love of country and attachment to their General sustained them under their unparalleled hardships; with any other leader, the army would have dissolved and vanished."[141]

Washington's character and encouragement inspired the army to follow his example, and his heart was devoted to his men as well as to his country. From the beginning, he tirelessly traveled throughout the camp, his presence bringing strength to the men. After observing his naked and distressed soldiers, he said: "I feel superabundantly for them, and from my Soul pity those miseries, wch. it is neither in my power to relieve or prevent."[142]

Washington knew that the cause for which they fought was worth any price—even the suffering at Valley Forge—for they purchased liberty not only for themselves but for the generations to come. But at Valley Forge, blood was not shed in battle, and still the army shed much blood. "The blood that stained this ground," wrote Henry Brown, "did not rush forth in the joyous frenzy of the fight; it fell drop by drop from the heart of a suffering people. They who once encamped here in the snow fought not for conquest, not for power, not for glory, not for their country only, not for themselves alone. They served here for Posterity; they suffered here for the Human Race; they bore here the cross of all the peoples; they died here that freedom might be the heritage of all."[143]

If Washington's character helped to sustain the army, one must ask, What sustained Washington? This question could easily be answered by Washington's soldiers, because they knew his trust was in God. The army had frequently received orders from its general to attend church and to observe days of prayer and fasting and days of thanksgiving. Plus he had secured chaplains for the army. Henry Muhlenberg recalled how Washington "rode around among his army . . . and admonished each and every one to fear God, to put away the wickedness that has set in and become so general, and to practice the Christian virtues."[144]

Almost every man in the army personally knew that his general "regularly attends divine service in his tent every morning and evening, and seems very fervent in his prayers."[145] Henry Knox was one who recounted that Washington frequently visited secluded groves to lay the cause of his bleeding country at the throne of grace.[146]

A number of people recounted the story of Isaac Potts, a Tory Quaker, who came upon Washington while he was on his knees in prayer in the woods. G. W. P. Custis related that Potts later remarked to his wife: "If there is anyone on this earth whom the Lord will listen to, it is George Washington; and I feel a presentiment that under such a commander there can be no doubt of our eventually establishing our independence, and that God in his providence has willed it so."[147]

In this most difficult of times, Washington constantly relied upon God and trusted in Him for success. God was faithful to answer his prayers, and through Washington, He eventually established America's independence and secured the beginning of the most free and prosperous nation the world has ever seen.

How did God answer Washington's prayers? One miracle occurred that winter that helped to eliminate the army's situation of near starving. Bruce Lancaster described the event: "One foggy morning the soldiers noticed the Schuylkill River seemed to be boiling. The disturbance was caused by thousands and thousands of shad which were making their way upstream in an unusually early migration. With pitchforks and shovels, the men plunged into the water, throwing the fish onto the banks. [Henry] Lee's dragoons rode their horses into the stream to keep the shad from swimming on out of reach. Suddenly and wonderfully, there was plenty of food for the army."[148]

God's providence could also be seen in the arrival of Friedrich von Steuben at Valley Forge on February 23. No one could have been more valuable at the time, for he trained and drilled the men into a well-disciplined army. His rigorous instruction gave the troops confidence in themselves as soldiers even as Washington had given them confidence as men. Not only had godly character and strength been forged and tempered within the army, but military skill had also been imparted to them at last.

Another providential event occurred that winter when France became an ally to America. This meant much-needed money and additional troops would pour into the new nation. The Continental Congress acknowledged this as the hand of God when the representatives declared a national day of thanksgiving on May 7, 1778. At Valley Forge on May 5, Washington proclaimed: "It having pleased the Almighty ruler of the Universe propitiously to defend the Cause of the United American States and finally by raising up a powerful Friend among the Princes of the Earth to establish our liberty and Independence upon lasting foundations, it becomes us to set apart a day for gratefully acknowledging the divine Goodness and celebrating the important Event which we owe to his benign Interposition."[149]

The troops' survival, the molding of a disciplined army, Washington's amazing leadership, and all the miraculous occurrences during the winter at Valley Forge can only be attributed to almighty God. Washington certainly acknowledged Him in the events of the war, writing: "The man must be bad indeed who can look upon the events of the American Revolution without feeling the warmest gratitude towards the great Author of the Universe whose divine interposition was so frequently manifested in our behalf."[150]

The Providence of God

*By these great qualities, and their benign effects,
has Providence marked out the Head of this
Nation, with a hand so distinctly visible, as to
have been seen by all men, and mistaken by none.*

—John Adams

*I*N A FAMOUS ORATION, Henry Lee asserted that
Washington was "designed by Heaven" to lead
in the affairs of the birth of America, adding, "The finger
of an overruling Providence pointing at Washington was
neither mistaken nor unobserved."[151] Early Americans believed in the providence of God and saw His hand clearly
in Washington's life. And Washington himself was a firm
believer in Providence.

Noah Webster was an acquaintance of Washington and
even visited Mount Vernon. In his dictionary, Webster de-
fines *providence* as "the care and superintendence which
God exercises over his creatures," and he points out that
belief in a general providence necessitates a belief in a
particular providence.[152] God governs in His creation in
general and directs the overall affairs of men to fulfill His
overall purpose for mankind; but He does so by sover-

eignly moving in the lives of individuals, enabling them to fulfill their personal destiny. The two are of necessity linked, for "a *general providence* consists of particulars." Events of history have not happened by chance but by God's choice to fulfill His plan for the nations. One's personal destiny is part of God's overall plan, and what happens in the lives of individuals often has great effect on the course of history. Such was the life of Washington. This providential man impacted the history of America and the advancement of liberty in the world.

Washington wrote of the providence of God scores of times in his public and private writings. He not only believed in a general Providence, he also embraced a particular Providence. He believed that God not only oversaw the workings of His creation in a general sense, but He moved specifically in small and large events to accomplish His will and purposes. This was seen numerous times in the course of the Revolutionary War. For example, when Arnold's treason was discovered, Washington attributed this to the providence of God. In addition to Washington's words mentioned before (in Part 1), he wrote the president of Congress: "That over-ruling Providence which has so often, and so remarkably interposed in our favor, never manifested itself more conspicuously than in the timely discovery of his horrid design of surrendering the Post and Garrison of West point into the hands of the enemy."[153]

He not only often spoke of Providence, but his life demonstrated the hand of God in preserving and directing him. He also demonstrated a personal reliance upon the providence of God through a calm, sure dependence upon the divine aid. The first part of this book outlined the providential preparation of Washington in his early life—from the training of his parents, to contracting smallpox, to protection during the French and Indian War. His first engagement in that war concluded with ten of the enemy killed, one wounded, and twenty-one captured, but the colonists, Washington wrote, "had only one Man kill'd, and two or three wounded, . . . a most miraculous escape, as Our Right Wing was much expos'd to their Fire and receiv'd it all."[154] And he was in the middle of the heaviest fire—"The right wing, where I stood, was exposed to and received all the enemy's fire"—but "I fortunately excaped."[155] His providential protection at the battle of the Monongahela in 1775 was even more dramatic.

God's providence was seen in material provision as well. Washington wrote in 1754: "We have not provisions of any sort enough in camp to serve us two days. Once before we should have been four days without provisions, if Providence had not sent a trader from the Ohio to our relief."[156]

After Congress chose Washington to be the commander of the army, he wrote to Martha from Philadelphia, explaining that he did not have time to return to Mount Vernon but must go to Boston to take charge of the army. In his June 18, 1775, letter, he said, "I shall rely, therefore, confidently on that Providence, which has heretofore preserved and been bountiful to me, not doubting but that I shall return safe to you in the fall."[157] He wrote again on June 23, 1775: "I go fully trusting in that providence, which has been more bountiful to me than I deserve and in full confidence of a happy meeting with you some time in the fall."[158]

The general was providentially protected many times in battle. In the fall of 1777 during the battle of Brandywine, British Capt. Patrick Ferguson had an interesting encounter with Washington, which he described in a letter to a kinsman. His riflemen were lying in hiding "when a Rebel officer, remarkable by a hussar dress, passed towards our army, within a hundred yards of my right flank, not perceiving us." Another officer was with this man. Ferguson ordered three men to fire upon the unsuspecting officers, but "the idea disgusting me, I recalled the order." The officers circled around, with the most eminent one approaching within a hundred yards of Ferguson, who stepped out from hiding and called for him to stop. The American officer stopped, looked at Ferguson, but then proceeded, whereupon, Ferguson called again,

> levelling my piece at him; but he slowly cantered away. As I was within that distance, at which, in the quickest firing, I could have lodged half a dozen balls in or about him, before he was out of my reach, I had only to determine; but it was not pleasant to fire at the back of an unoffending individual, who was acquitting himself very coolly of his duty—so I let him alone. The day after, I had been telling this story to some wounded officers who lay in the same room with me, when one of the surgeons, who had been dressing the wounded Rebel officers, came in, and told us, that they had been informing him that General Washington was all the morning with the light troops, and only attended by a French officer in hussar dress, he himself dressed and mounted in every point as

above described. I am not sorry that I did not know at the time who it was.[159]

Had Washington fallen, the cause of the Americans may well have died with him. Historian Lyman Draper said of this incident: "This singular impulse of Ferguson, illustrates, in a forcible manner, the over-ruling hand of Providence in directing the operation of a man's mind when he himself is least of all aware of it."[160]

Many officers and soldiers acknowledged God's providential protection upon Washington during the war. Witnessing events during the battle of Monmouth, Dr. James Craik, who had been with Washington in 1770 when the Indian chief gave his prophecy, said to some officers: "Gentlemen, recollect what I have often told you, of the old Indian's prophecy. Yes, I do believe, a Great Spirit protects that man—and that one day or other, honored and beloved, he will be the chief of our nation, as he is now our general, our father, and our friend. Never mind the enemy, they can not kill him, and while he lives, our cause will never die."[161]

God's providence was manifested in many other ways during the war. For instance, Washington was preserved from an attempted poisoning. While he was in New York City in 1776, one of his life guards (select officers assigned to protect the general) placed poison in a dish of peas that was prepared for the general's table. Washington's housekeeper, the daughter of his steward Samuel Fraunces, exposed this attempt and saved the general's life.[162]

Weather was a factor many times during the war, seemingly always benefiting the American cause. At the beginning of the war, while Washington fortified Dorchester Heights, "the red-coats were prevented," John C. Fitzpatrick wrote, "from crossing the water by a sudden and violent storm which lasted so long that by the time it was over [British Gen. William] Howe felt that the works had become too strong for him, gave over the attempt and evacuated the town."[163] Of this incident, Washington wrote to his brother John, "That this remarkable interposition of Providence is for some wise purpose, I have not a doubt."[164]

Another incident affected by weather occurred in August 1776. During the fighting on Long Island, Howe and his army of thirty-two thousand men had inflicted heavy losses on the Continental army but had not succeeded in capturing or destroying it. Howe then prepared to attack the eight thousand American troops on Brooklyn Heights.

The British army had surrounded Washington's troops in a great semicircle, with their backs to the nearly mile-wide East River. Howe held this position for two days and did not attack. Had he struck, victory would have been certain for the superior numbers of the British force. Washington realized that to fight would mean defeat and the likely end of the war. Surrender was unthinkable. As difficult as it would be, he decided to retreat across the East River since all land routes were blocked by the British. The Continental army could have easily been surrounded by the British, but providentially, adverse weather conditions kept British ships from sailing up the East River. As a result, the Continentals were able to escape.

To make sure the British did not discover their retreat, Washington evacuated his army in great secrecy, even from his own troops. He sent orders for every rowboat, sailboat, and seagoing vessel in the area to be collected. At eight o'clock on the night of August 29, 1776, the evacuation began in a heavy rain; adverse winds hindered the British ships from attempting any activity. In this weather, the sailboats were of little use, and only the few rowboats were employed in the retreat. But at the rate at which the oarsmen could work, a successful evacuation seemed impossible. At eleven o'clock that evening, however, the northeast wind that had been raging for three days amazingly stopped, and the water became so calm that the boats could be loaded with extra weight. A gentle breeze also blew in from the south and southwest, which favored the Continentals' progress across the river to New York.

Yet as the adverse weather changed, a new problem was created. Under the light of a full moon, the British were sure to see the movement of the American troops. Miraculously, though, the Continentals retreated all night without being heard or seen.

The retreat continued through the darkness of the predawn, but as the sun began to rise, many troops were yet to be evacuated. Death seemed imminent. Maj. Benjamin Tallmadge, who was still on the island, recorded what happened in his memoirs:

> As the dawn of the next day approached, those of us who remained in the trenches became very anxious for our own safety, and when the dawn appeared there were several regiments still on duty. At this time a very dense fog began to rise (out of the ground and off the river) and it seemed to settle in a peculiar manner over both encampments.

I recall this peculiar providential occurrence perfectly well, and so very dense was the atmosphere that I could scarcely discern a man at six yards distance. . . . We tarried until the sun had risen, but the fog remained as dense as ever.[165]

The fog remained until the last boats left Long Island.

Another miraculous event occurred during this retreat, and Washington Irving described it in his *Life of Washington.* Near the ferry where the troops were being evacuated, a family lived who favored the British cause. Upon seeing the army's embarkation, the lady of the house sent a servant to alert the British to what was happening. The servant managed to slip past the American guards, but upon reaching the British lines, he halted at an outpost of German-speaking mercenaries and was unable to communicate with them. The servant was put under guard until the next morning, when a British officer questioned him. Upon hearing the news of the American evacuation, some Redcoats were sent to confirm the report. They cautiously approached the Continental camp only to find it empty.

British troops hurried to the river. As they arrived, the fog lifted enough for them to see four boats on the East River. The only boat near enough to be captured contained three vagabonds who had lingered in the camp to plunder it. Otherwise, eight thousand men, with nearly all their supplies, had miraculously retreated to New York.

American Gen. Nathanael Greene called the withdrawal from Long Island "the best effected retreat I ever read or heard of."[166] This extraordinary retreat was one of the most improbable and important events of the war, and many attributed the fortunate series of events to "a peculiar Providence."[167]

Weather was a factor many other times. On October 28, 1776, a superior British force drove the Continentals from the field at White Plains, New York, and would have pressed their advantage, but a sudden heavy rain rendered any continued operation impossible.[168] The crossing of the Delaware and Washington's victory at Trenton, the miraculous retreat from Cowpens and through the Carolinas, and the battle of Yorktown were all greatly influenced by weather.[169]

After Washington retired as commander of the army, he wrote to Gen. Henry Knox in February 1784 and remarked on his adjustment to private life: "I feel now, however, as I conceive a wearied Traveller must do, who, after treading many a painful step, with a heavy burden on his shoulders, is eased of the latter, having reached the Goal to which all the former were directed; and from his House top is looking back, and tracing with a grateful eye the Meanders by which he escaped the quicksands and Mires which lay in his way; and into which none but the All-powerful guide, and great disposer of human Events could have prevented his falling."[170]

Washington was always an optimist, believing that God, in His providence, would see His cause prevail. This belief sustained him during the great difficulties of the war. Even if things did not seem to be going favorably, he still recognized that God was at work fulfilling His plan. He knew there would be struggles, defeats, setbacks, and hardships, but in the end, those who stood for right would succeed: "Happy, happy, thrice happy country, if such were the government of it! But, alas! We are not to expect that the path is to be strewed with flowers. That great and good Being who rules the universe has disposed matters otherwise, and for wise purposes I am persuaded."[171]

To his friend Bryan Fairfax, Washington wrote: "The determinations of Providence are all ways wise; often inscrutable, and though its decrees appear to bear hard upon us at times is nevertheless meant for gracious purposes."[172]

Washington's view of the providence of God is summarized well in his reply to a letter from the Reverend John Rodgers, who had congratulated him on the victory in the American Revolution: "I accept, with much pleasure your kind Congratulations on the happy Event of Peace, with the Establishment of our Liberties and Independence. Glorious indeed has been our Contest: glorious, if we consider the Prize for which we have contended, and glorious in its Issue; but in the midst of our Joys, I hope we shall not forget that, to divine Providence is to be ascribed the Glory and the Praise."[173]

Throughout his life, Washington consistently acknowledged God's providence and gave Him the glory and praise for things great and small.

SELF-GOVERNMENT

It is our duty, to make the best of our misfortunes, and not suffer passion to interfere with our interest and the public good.

$\mathcal{G}$EORGE WASHINGTON WAS STRONG in character, and he also had strong emotions. He was a passionate man, but he usually kept his passions in control. As a young man, his passions were more likely to erupt, but as he grew older, he learned to keep them in check. He wrote, "It is our duty to make the best of our misfortunes, and not to suffer passion to interfere with our interest and the public good."[174] He learned to govern himself, and this is why he was mighty. Thomas Jefferson observed, "His temper was naturally irritable and high-toned; but reflection and resolution had obtained a firm and habitual ascendency over it."[175]

His self-government was seen in his moderation and dress. Washington hated excess of any kind. He was very neat. He did not like tobacco, partially because it was messy, which was one reason he ceased to grow it as a cash crop and instead cultivated wheat and grains.

Washington not only controlled his own passions and life, he also exercised self-control in using various civil and military powers given to him. Toward the end of 1776, after being pushed out of New York and New Jersey through a series of defeats, and facing a great depletion of his army through the expirations of short-term enlistments, Washington asked Congress for new powers to restructure the military, without which he believed defeat would occur. Some feared this might result in a military dictatorship, or at least dangerously diminish the scope of the representative government. In a letter to Congress, the general wrote: "It may be said that this is an application for powers that are too dangerous to be Intrusted. I can only add, that desperate diseases require desperate Remedies; and with truth declare, that I have no lust after power but wish with as much fervency as any Man upon this wide extended Continent, for an oppertunity of turning the Sword in to a plow share. But . . . no person ever had a greater choice of difficulties to contend with than I have."[176]

Nathanael Greene wrote Congress, "There never was a Man that might be more safely trusted, nor a Time when there was a louder Call."[177] Congress entrusted the requested powers to Washington because the representatives had a "perfect reliance on the wisdom, vigor, and uprightness of General Washington."[178] The Congress wrote to him: "Happy is it for this country that the general of their forces can safely be intrusted with the most unlimited power, and neither personal security, liberty nor property, be in the least degree endangered thereby."[179] To this,

Washington replied that it was an honor to be trusted with powers "almost unlimited in extent," which did not free him from "civil obligations" but that constantly reminded him that "as the Sword was the last Resort for the preservation of our Liberties, so it ought to be the first thing laid aside, when those Liberties are firmly established."[180] Washington proved himself by exercising his authority in a responsible and positive way, as well as readily laying down his powers at the end of hostilities.

In this, as well as when he was charting new powers as president, he never used more power than was necessary to accomplish the ends for which it was given. His desire was not to wield power but to serve his country and advance the cause of liberty.

There are a few instances when Washington lost his self-restraint for a moment, though always bring it under control in the end. One of those occurred at the battle of Monmouth, when Washington encountered Gen. Charles Lee, who had ordered a retreat contrary to orders.

"What is the meaning of all this, sir?" Washington exclaimed fiercely to Lee.

When Lee hesitated, Washington's anger rose and he demanded an explanation. When Lee replied angrily without answering the question, Washington called him "a damned poltroon," which meant coward or a wretch who lacked spirit or courage. Lafayette later said, "This was the only time I ever heard General Washington swear."[181]

This rare loss of restraint, considering the great trials and obstacles he faced, is a testament to Washington's self-government. Summarizing this character trait, biographer Jared Sparks said: "His passions were strong, and sometimes they broke out with vehemence, but he had the power of checking them in an instant. Perhaps self-control was the most remarkable trait of his character."[182]

A text suggested for use on an early monument to Washington declared, "His noblest Victory the Conquest of himself."[183] True power resides with those who have learned to govern themselves. Proverbs 16:32 says that "he who rules his spirit" is mightier "than he who takes a city." This is what made Washington a powerful man.

OBEDIENCE

The very idea of the power and the right of the people to establish Government, presupposes the duty of every individual to obey the established Government.

*T*HE TRAINING BY WASHINGTON'S parents provided him the essential qualities necessary to accomplish his destiny to lead. Washington was born to rule, and of first importance in preparation for this was his learning to obey. Obedience is that quality necessary in anyone who desires to live free. There can be no liberty in a nation where there is not first a spirit of obedience. Obedience begins in the home, and it underlies all the qualities that make for a good son, a good soldier, and a good citizen. *Poor Richard's Almanac* recorded the primary importance of obedience: "Let thy child's first lesson be obedience, and the second will be what thy wilt."

Obedience is the habit of submitting one's will and actions to that which is right. God is the ultimate determiner of what is right, but when a person is young, his or her parents stand in the place of God. Thus, living a life of obedience to God and earthly authorities begins by learning to obey one's parents. Godly obedience entails not just outward action but internal submission of the heart.

Washington was taught from a young age not only to obey but to obey cheerfully. At age fourteen he received a warrant to be a British midshipman, much like his brother Lawrence had been. Indeed, Washington sought the position because his brother had been in the navy. Washington was eager to embark on this profession, but his mother objected. He had sent his clothes to the ship, but when he came to see how opposed his mother was to his going to sea, he dutifully obeyed her wishes without any complaining. He obeyed cheerfully. The request of his mother certainly was providential. Washington's quality of obedience, which appeared to him at the time to relegate him to life on the farm, assured he would be taking the path that would lead him to become the leader of the American cause of liberty.[184]

His prompt and faithful obedience to his parents prepared him to be a good military man, which at times required obedience to unwise orders. During the French and Indian War, he was told to lead his troops through a new trail being cut in the wilderness, instead of using the already existing trail cut previously by Braddock's troops. He expressed strenuous opposition to this plan but performed his duty, obeying his Commander from within. (Washington's views proved to be the better course of action.) Because he acted this way, the Virginians succeeded in their endeavors to capture Fort Duquesne (though this could have been done sooner with less toil had Washington's plan been followed).[185]

Washington was entrusted with great authority because he was a man under authority. As commanding general, he never tried to usurp the authority of the Congress. He saw Congress and the states as the source of his authority. He wrote to them requests when he had needs. He did not demand, but rather sought their permission. Even when he was hindered in performing his duties by the many attempts of Congress to dictate military matters, he operated in a spirit of obedience. This quality in the commander of the army convinced Congress to give Washington almost unlimited powers when the legislature was forced to flee Philadelphia and the cause looked bleak. Washington could have assumed the power of a dictator, but he used his power to accomplish greater things for the cause—victories at Trenton and Princeton, and he drove the British out of most of New Jersey. He then returned the emergency powers entrusted to him, gladly submitting to Congress's authority.

As Washington obeyed others, so his troops obeyed him. Washington records that during the great hardships at Valley Forge, the troops "submitting without a murmur, is a mark of patience and obedience which in my opinion can scarce be parallel'd."[186]

Washington obeyed men, but he also obeyed his conscience. He spent his life obeying that sense of right within him.

BIBLICAL WORLDVIEW

I am sure, the mass of citizens in these United States mean well; and I firmly believe they will always act well, whenever they can obtain a right understanding of matters.

$\mathcal{G}$OOD CIVIL LEADERS SHOULD have not only excellent character but also knowledge of the truth, especially in regard to public affairs and governmental philosophy. The Founders believed that they should view all of life from a biblical perspective; that is, they should have a biblical worldview. How one thinks determines how one acts. A leader will govern based upon his presuppositions of law, government, economics, liberty, and life. If these presuppositions are rooted in relativism, humanism, secularism, statism, or positivism, the fruit will not be life, liberty, prosperity, or virtue. If they are rooted in true religion and morality, according to Washington, the fruit will be personal and political freedom and prosperity.

It would take many books to examine Washington's worldview. This brief summary shows, however, his underlying beliefs were rooted in the eternal absolutes of the

Holy Scriptures, which formed the foundation of Western civilization and the American Republic.

George Washington understood what was necessary to build a free nation. In his Farewell Address of 1796, he wrote: "Of all the dispositions and habits which lead to political prosperity, religion and morality are indispensable supports.—In vain would that man claim the tribute of Patriotism, who should labour to subvert these great Pillars of human happiness, these firmest props of the duties of man and Citizens."[187] To address the mistaken view of the French revolutionaries, Washington added: "And let us with caution indulge the supposition, that morality can be maintained without religion. . . . [R]eason and experience both forbid us to expect, that national morality can prevail in exclusion of religious principle."[188]

To Washington and the Founders, true religion was Christianity.[189] It was the Christian religion, and the morality that flowed from this, that produced liberty, happiness, and prosperity.[190] The "politician" as well as "the pious man, ought to respect and to cherish them." He had written earlier that the "practice of the moral and religious obligations, are the strongest claims to national and individual happiness."[191] He reiterated this idea in 1797, writing, "Religion and Morality are the essential pillars of Civil society."[192]

Washington's role in the birth of liberty in the United States is magnified when it is realized that the success of the new experiment in a republican model of government in America would determine the advance of liberty and free governments in the future. The Earl of Buchan wrote, "The preservation of the sacred fire of liberty and the destiny of the republican model of government are justly considered as deeply, perhaps finally, staked on the experiment entrusted to the hands of the American people."[193] Washington's work in securing and advancing liberty in America determined the advance of liberty in the world. Without Washington, American liberty would not have been realized, and consequently the advance of liberty in the past two hundred years would have been stifled or would not have occurred as it did. This is why Thomas Paine called him "the world's apostle of liberty."

The goal of the American Revolution was liberty. In an invitation to Canada to join the American cause, Washington wrote: "We have taken up Arms in Defence of our Liberty, our Property; our Wives and our Children: We are determined to preserve them or die. . . . The cause of America and of liberty is the cause of every virtuous American Citizen Whatever may be his Religion or his descent."[194]

Washington advanced the cause of liberty, all types of liberty—civil, religious, personal, or economic. In orders to his troops, he wrote, "It is for the preservation of his own Rights, Liberty and Property, and those of his Fellow Countrymen, that he is now called into service," thus he required the officers to "be exceeding diligent and strict in preventing all Invasions and Abuse of private property in their quarters."[195] According to Washington, private property rights are foundational for economic and civil liberty.

Washington believed that liberty has its origin in true religion. He also recognized certain governmental principles were necessary to support liberty. One of these was that power should lie with the people, not the rulers. He wrote to British Gen. Thomas Gage, August 20, 1775, that "a brave and free people [is] the purest source and original fountain of all power."[196] Rulers were not the source of authority, law, or liberty; they were merely representatives of the people. Authority flowed from the Author of liberty to men, who then delegated limited civil authority to rulers. Civil government has an important but limited role in advancing and preserving liberty. The civil government of a nation is to protect the life, liberty, and property of its citizens, but it must not abuse power. Washington wrote, "Government being, among other purposes, instituted to protect the persons and consciences of men from oppression, it certainly is the duty of rulers, not only to abstain from it themselves, but, according to their stations, to prevent it in others."[197]

Civil government, to Washington, was to be very limited. It was not to have all power to regulate and control every aspect of life. He demonstrated this view every time he was placed in a position of leadership, never exercising more authority than was necessary to accomplish his delegated role. He even went beyond this, refusing any pay as general and, as president, refusing housing that was provided at public expense.[198] He set a proper example of the role of president by living in a modest home, which greatly contrasted with the practice of European kings. He wrote to Martha, "The example of the President and his family will render parade and expense improper and disreputable."[199] He had no thought of holding on to power, either as general or as president. He set the precedent in the American experience for the peaceful transfer of power.

Washington was a firm proponent of the rights of conscience and religious liberty, and he saw the American government as a protector of freedom of worship. In 1789, he wrote to the United Baptist Churches in Virginia:

> If I could have entertained the slightest apprehension, that the constitution framed in the convention, where I had the honor to preside, might possibly endanger the religious rights of any ecclesiastical society, certainly I would never have placed my signature to it; and, if I could now conceive that the general government might ever be so administered as to render the liberty of conscience insecure, I beg you will be persuaded, that no one would be more zealous than myself to establish effectual barriers against the horrors of spiritual tyranny, and every species of religious persecution. For you doubtless remember, that I have often expressed my sentiments, that every man, conducting himself as a good citizen, and being accountable to God alone for his religious opinions, ought to be protected in worshipping the Deity according to the dictates of his own conscience.[200]

Though Washington was a Protestant, and he believed those who embraced other doctrines were in error, he valued the rights of conscience of all people and maintained that none should be violated. When Benedict Arnold led American troops into Canada during the Revolution, Washington sent him instructions on September 14, 1775, regarding his actions, which included: "I also give it in Charge to you to avoid all Disrespect to or Contempt of the Religion of the Country and its Ceremonies. Prudence, Policy, and a true Christian Spirit, will lead us to look with Compassion upon their Errors without insulting them. While we are contending for our own Liberty, we should be very cautious of violating the Rights of Conscience in others, ever considering that God alone is the Judge of the Hearts of Men, and to him only in this Case, they are answerable."[201]

Around this same time, he wrote of "that ridiculous and childish custom of burning the Effigy of the pope," which some troops stationed with the army around Boston were doing, expressing his surprise that there were any people in the army "so void of common sense." He added, "At such a juncture, and in such Circumstances, to be insulting their Religion [the people of Canada], is so monstrous, as not to be suffered or excused."[202]

Religious liberty was of central importance to Washington, who wrote to the Quakers in 1789, "The liberty enjoyed by the people of these States, of worshipping Almighty God agreeably to their consciences, is not only among the choicest of their blessings, but also of their rights."[203]

Washington believed education was essential because it provided a foundation of usefulness and happiness for the future. He wrote to G. W. P. Custis "of the propriety and necessity of devoting your youthful days in the acquirement of that knowledge which will be advantageous, grateful, and pleasing to you in maturer years, and may be the foundation of your usefulness here, and happiness hereafter."[204]

Washington saw education as a means to benefit both the individual who learned and the nation at large. He wrote to the president of St. John's College in Annapolis, Maryland, how he must lead Custis "in the best manner . . . to the study of such useful acquirements as may be serviceable to himself, and eventually, beneficial to his Country."[205]

The education Washington received from his mother, father, brother, and others prepared him to live a productive and useful life, one benefiting him, his nation, and God's higher purposes. This is what he sought to provide for those under his care and influence, as seen in his many letters to Martha's children and grandchildren and to his nephews and other relatives. His epistles contain much instruction on many subjects, including business, love, character traits, and politics.

That men have a right to use force of arms as a last resort to secure their rights and liberties was a belief Washington held early on, writing in April 1769: "That no man shou'd scruple, or hesitate a moment, to use arms in defence of so valuable a blessing . . . is clearly my opinion; yet Arms, I wou'd beg leave to add, should be the last resource."[206]

On December 3, 1793, in his fifth annual address to Congress, Washington laid out his view of peace through strength. "There is a rank due to the United States among Nations," he wrote, "which will be withheld, if not absolutely lost, by the reputation of weakness. If we desire to avoid insult, we must be able to repel it; if we desire to secure peace, one of the most powerful instruments of our rising prosperity, it must be known, that we are at all times ready for War."[207]

While Washington believed the cause of America in the struggle for independence was righteous, he knew God would be the final judge. In a response to British Gen. Thomas Gage, who commanded the troops in Boston in the summer of 1775, Washington wrote: "May that God, to whom you then appealed, judge between America and you."[208]

COURAGE

I have a constitution hardy enough to encounter and undergo the most severe tryals; and, I flatter myself, resolution to face what any man durst, as shall be prov'd when it comes to the test.

THOMAS JEFFERSON SAID THAT Washington "was incapable of fear, meeting personal dangers with the calmest unconcern."[209] He demonstrated great courage throughout his life: from his travels as a surveyor, including encountering many Indians, to his trip to deliver the Virginia governor's message to the French, to his action in the French and Indian War, he showed no fear as a young man. He wrote at this time, "I have a Constitution hardy enough to encounter and undergo the most severe tryals, and, I flatter myself, resolution to Face what any Man durst, as shall be prov'd when it comes to the Test."[210]

He once discovered an intruder who was poaching game on his farm and confronted him with the least concern for his safety, even though the interloper had a gun aimed at him.[211] He strongly supported action for independence without fear of repercussion.

During the Revolutionary War, Washington was often in the midst of battle, with gun and artillery fire all around him, yet he never showed any fear or concern for his own personal safety. When the British attacked Kipp's Bay on September 15, 1776, the greatly outnumbered Continentals fled in confusion, giving no heed to their superiors who attempted to stop their retreat. When Washington received word of this, he galloped in the midst of his flying troops, shouting to them to turn and face the enemy. After this proved useless, his passions greatly aroused, he drew his sword to rally the troops and then halted his horse in the midst of enemy fire with pistols drawn. One of his aides, fearing for his life, seized his bridle and forced him from the spot.[212]

During the battle at Princeton on January 3, 1777, Washington rode into the thick of battle to rally his retreating troops. When this initially failed, he exposed himself directly to the enemy by riding up and down the line, setting an example of fearlessness to his men. When one of his aides, Col. John Fitzgerald, saw him, he covered his eyes for fear of seeing him fall. Yet after another volley of British muskets, this man whom many believed was protected by Providence, still sat upon his horse, now with the men rallying at his presence. Fitzgerald rode to Washington's side and exclaimed, "Thank God! Your excellency is safe."[213] Washington, always calm even amid the chaos of battle, ordered Fitzgerald to bring up the troops, declaring, "The day is our own."[214]

At the battle of Germantown, when the Continentals broke and began to retreat just at the moment of victory, Washington exerted all his effort to rally the troops, fearlessly exposing himself to enemy fire. When his officers failed to persuade him to move, they had to seize the bridle of his horse. Gen. John Sullivan wrote: "I saw our brave commander-in-chief exposing himself to the hottest fire of the enemy in such a manner, that regard for my country obliged me to ride to him and beg him to retire. He, to gratify me and some others, withdrew to a small distance, but his anxiety for the fate of the day soon brought him up again, where he remained till our troops had retreated."[215]

On May 28, 1778, the Continental army engaged the British at Monmouth Court House in New Jersey. Gen. Charles Lee was given orders to lead the bulk of the army against the middle of the British lines; he would be supported on both sides. Washington was miles behind with reinforcements. But as Washington approached the battlefield, he received word that the army was retreating, to which he exclaimed, "Impossible!" He quickly rode forward, seeking to talk with Lee. As recounted earlier, this conversation was one of the few instances that Washington lost his temper in public. He assumed command of Lee's retreating troops and rallied the men, repairing his broken line. He was indefatigable, but his horse was not, and the animal died underneath him. Washington leaped on another, calling out, "Stand fast, my boys! And receive your enemy."[216]

Lafayette described Washington on the battlefield that day: "At Monmouth I commanded a division, and it may be supposed was pretty well occupied; still I took time, amid the roar and confusion of the conflict, to admire our beloved chief, who rode along the lines, mounted on a splendid charger, amid the shouts of the soldiers, cheering them by his voice and example, and restoring the fortunes of the flight. I thought then, as now, that I never had beheld so superb a man."[217]

At one point, a British cannonball landed so near Washington's horse that dirt was thrown all over the general. Still, he was not harmed. Some who witnessed this were reinforced in their idea that Washington was under the protection of Providence and could not be harmed—that this was in accordance with the prophecy of the Indian chief from the French and Indian War: "The Great Spirit protects him, he cannot die in battle."[218]

Washington showed his fearlessness at the battle of Yorktown as well, constantly exposing himself to enemy fire as he stood on parapets and reconnoitered the enemy's works. During one such moment, an officer was killed only yards away from the general.[219]

Washington was almost too courageous. His fearlessness brought some uneasiness among the troops. An officer wrote in 1777: "Our army love their General very much, but they have one thing against him, which is the little care he takes of himself in any action. His personal bravery, and the desire he has of animating his troops by example, make him fearless of danger. This occasions us much uneasiness. But Heaven, which has hitherto been his shield, I hope will still continue to guard so valuable a life."[220]

DUTY AND SERVICE

*As the Congress desire it, I will enter upon the
momentous duty, and exert every power I
possess, in their service, and for the support of
the glorious cause.*

SERVICE WAS WASHINGTON'S MOTTO. He served his
family, wife, friends, strangers, parish, state,
and nation. Duty motivated Washington to spend forty
years of his life in public service. After retiring as general
after the Revolutionary War, he never intended to enter
public life again. His desire was to retire to Mount Vernon
and exert his energies to see it prosper. However, when
his country called for him at the Constitutional Convention and then to be president, "an honest conviction of
duty superseded my former resolution," and he answered
the call.[221]

His strong sense of duty can be seen early in his life.
Anticipating the attack at Fort Necessity in 1754 by a
much larger French force, he wrote to Virginia governor
Dinwiddie: "And this is as much as I can promise, but my
best endeavour's shall not be wanting to deserve more, I

doubt not if you hear I am beaten, but you will at the same [time,] hear that we have done our duty in fighting as long [as] there was a possibility of hope."[222]

They were attacked and eventually surrendered to the larger force, but Washington's command performed its duty by fighting as long as possible. Washington also would perform his duty throughout his life, regardless of the potential for defeat; win or lose, he always acted as he should.

Washington's words and actions throughout the Revolutionary War confirm that his motivation for service was not self-seeking but rather a desire to advance the cause of liberty. Many times he was presented with opportunities for more power, but he always put these aside.

Many people have said that Washington embodied the Revolution because the country probably would not have won the struggle for independence without his leadership. He was not only instrumental in winning the war, but he also thwarted an attempt to establish a monarchy. His action in rejecting some officers' attempts to make him king shows his desire to serve his country rather than rule it. Shortly after this monarchical effort, Washington was instrumental in quashing a military coup.

Ten months after Washington wrote to Col. Lewis Nicola, urging him to consider a constitutional means of resolving the problems facing them, a circular calling for a military revolt began appearing among the army. To avert national turmoil, Washington met with his officers on March 15, 1783, to hear their grievances. He let them know, however, that he strongly opposed any civil discord. After talking at length, the officers were still sullen and silent; his plea had failed to persuade them. Finally, he reached into his pocket and pulled out a letter. He told them that several congressmen were anxious to help, and he wanted to read a letter from them that described what was being planned. He held up the letter and tried to read the small writing. Biographer James Flexner described what followed:

> The officers stirred impatiently in their seats, and then suddenly every heart missed a beat. Something was the matter with His Excellency. He seemed unable to read the paper. He paused in bewilderment. He fumbled in his waistcoat pocket. And then he pulled out something that only his intimates had seen him wear. A pair of glasses. He explained, "Gentlemen, you will permit me to put on my spectacles, for I have not only grown gray but almost blind in the service of my country."
>
> This simple statement achieved what all Washington's rhetoric and all his arguments had been unable to achieve. The officers were instantly in tears, and from behind the shining drops, their eyes looked with love at the commander who had led them all so far and long.
>
> Washington quietly finished reading the congressman's letter, walked out of the hall, mounted his horse, and disappeared from the view of those who were staring from the window.[223]

All voted to support Washington for a peaceful, constructive approach to solve their problems (with one abstention). Historians point to this speech as pivotal. Thomas Jefferson wrote of Washington a year later, "The moderation and virtue of a single character have probably prevented this revolution from being closed, as most others have been, by a subversion of that liberty it was intended to establish."[224]

Writing to the president of Congress of the officers' action, Washington reported: "The result of the proceedings of the grand convention of officers, which I have the honor of enclosing . . . will, I flatter myself, be considered as the last glorious proof of patriotism which could have been given by men who aspired to the distinction of a patriot army; and will not only confirm their claim to the justice, but will increase their title to the gratitude, of their country."[225] Characteristically, he did not mention the part he played in the matter.

Four years later, Washington again played a key role in service to his country by presiding at the Constitutional Convention. He did not want to attend the convention, and in fact was just recovering from a serious illness. Nevertheless, when duty called, he responded. His presence and influence provided the stability necessary for the delegates to agree on a new constitution. Commenting on Washington's immense influence in the convention, James Monroe wrote to Jefferson on July 12, 1788: "Be assured General Washington's influence carried this government." He also assured its initial success by serving as the first president under the new Constitution.

Washington was unanimously elected as the first president of the United States, but he did not seek the office. He would have preferred to stay at his beloved Mount Vernon. He was advanced in age and was greatly enjoying retirement and "agricultural amusements." People knew of Washington's reluctance to serve again in public life, but they also knew of his strong sense of duty and willingness to sacrifice personal well-being for the public good. He wrote that, regardless of personal desires, he would serve if the people believed no one else could do it as well as he.[226] His obedience to his conscience—he did "what my conscience informed me was right, as it respected my God, my country, and myself"[227]—and the placement of the good of his country above his personal pleasure and reputation resulted in great blessing for America and the cause of liberty. His action assured the new nation would be established as a constitutional republic.

Washington's sense of duty and reliance upon God overcame his feelings of incompetence. As he traveled to New York to assume the presidency, he wrote to the citizens of Baltimore: "I know the delicate nature of the duties incident to the part which I am called to perform; and I feel my incompetence, without the singular assistance of Providence to discharge them in a satisfactory manner. But having undertaken the task, from a sense of duty, no fear of encountering difficulties and no dread of losing popularity, shall ever deter me from pursuing what I conceive to be the true interests of my Country."[228]

Having twice retired from public service, Washington was called upon again in 1798 by John Adams to be commander in chief of the provisional army of the United States to prepare for a possible conflict with France. G. W. P. Custis reflected the opinion of many concerning Washington's response to the call of duty: "I need not congratulate you on an appointment which was always designed by the Creator for one so fully capable of fulfilling it. Let an admiring world again behold a Cincinnatus springing up from rural retirement to the conquest of nations; and the future historian, in erasing so great a name, insert that of the 'Father of his country.'"[229]

America and the world should be thankful that Washington recognized and performed his obligations to his neighbor, his nation, and his God.

SACRIFICE IN SERVICE

I am growing old in my country's service, and losing my sight; but I never doubted its justice or its gratitude.

A GREAT CALLING REQUIRES great sacrifice. Washington fulfilled his calling and performed his duty and service to others only with much sacrifice. He gladly gave up personal interest and pleasure for the higher obligations he owed to God and country.

Washington spent almost all of his adult life serving his country in some capacity—six years in the Virginia militia, sixteen years as a member of the House of Burgesses, eight and a half years as general in chief, a member of the Constitutional Convention, and eight years as president. In addition, he served for many years as a vestryman, he served his children and relatives in many ways, and he served the myriads of visitors who sought him out after he became famous. Because of his service, he missed many years of what gave him the greatest pleasure: managing his estate with his family and friends around him. His farms and businesses suffered much from his absence.

At times his public service brought on severe illnesses. In the autumn of 1757, during a campaign against the French, he had to return home because of a bout of dysentery. This problem had bothered him for some time, but the condition grew so severe, his life was in danger. He needed more than four months to recover, during which time he was too weak to travel.[230] Many years later, while president, he became deathly ill as well.

His service brought unjust criticisms at times. During the war, most of the public did not understand the tenuous situation Washington faced, thus some complained about his inactivity and prudence. He could not let the public know the true condition of the army, as the enemy would benefit from such intelligence, therefore he resolutely received much criticism without response.

Much of Washington's service was without compensation. To avoid the appearance of personal gain from public calamities, and to give support to the cause, among other reasons, Washington declined all pay as general. But he worked diligently to secure proper payment for his troops. He wrote to the president of Congress on April 10, 1778, supporting increased compensation to officers, pointing out: "Personally, as an Officer, I have no interest in their decision, because I have declared, and now repeat it, that I never will receive the smallest benefit from the half pay establishment."[231] Just before he retired as general, the state of Pennsylvania offered him a stipend to help with the expenses that would accompany his great fame. He declined the offer.[232]

After the war, the state of Virginia wanted to compensate him in some way for his service. They voted him money, but he declined it. They issued him some stock in some newly formed companies, presenting this in a way that would not look like payment for his services, and even having it appear as an insult if he were to reject it. Even then, Washington accepted the stock only with the condition that he would donate any proceeds to charities. Some of these funds went to a school in Lexington, Virginia, that was renamed Washington College (present-day Washington and Lee University). Other funds went to support a school in the capital city.

Washington was prepared to give all for the cause of liberty and to perform his duties. He wrote in 1780: "No man had gone, and no man will go further to serve the public than myself. If sacrificing my whole estate would effect any valuable purpose, I would not hesitate one moment in doing it."[233] During the war, British ships sailed up the Potomac River and halted at Mount Vernon and demanded supplies. Washington's overseer, Lund Washington, honored their requests, hoping it would prevent them from destroying the general's home. When Washington heard what had done, he wrote Lund and said he would rather him burn everything than support the enemy: "I am very sorry to hear of your loss; I am a little sorry to hear of my own; but that which gives me most concern is, that you should go on board the enemy's vessels, and furnish them with refreshments. It would have been a less painful circumstance to me to have heard, that, in consequence of your non-compliance with their request, they had burnt my house and laid the plantation in ruins."[234]

Being away from his home was the pleasure Washington most missed. During his eight years as general of the army, from 1775 to 1783, he visited his beloved Mount Vernon only twice: a brief stay on his way to Yorktown in September 1781 and again after the surrender of Charles Cornwallis. He was often gone while serving as president as well.

Fulfilling the obligations to his high calling often took from him personal pleasures and preferences in relationships. It has been observed that a king can never have a friend, so Washington was often in a state of comparative isolation. Many held him in such high esteem that they felt they could not be close to him. In addition, Washington so often occupied himself with great concerns of his country that he had little time to pursue friendships.

Lund Washington once inquired how the general was to be rewarded for his service and great sacrifice after the war. The general replied: "There is one reward that nothing can deprive me of, and that is, the consciousness of having done my duty with the strictest rectitude, and most scrupulous exactness, and the certain knowledge, that if we should, ultimately, fail in the present contest, it is not owing to the want of exertion in me, or the application of every means that Congress and the United States, or the States individually, have put into my hands."[235]

Devotion and Loyalty to Family and Friends

*True friendship is a plant of slow growth, and
must undergo and withstand the shocks of
adversity, before it is entitled to the appellation.*

WHILE WASHINGTON WAS DEVOTED to his country and the cause of liberty, he did not let his lengthy service keep him from his devotion to his home, family, and friends. These were of first concern and delight to him. As president, he said, "I can truly say I had rather be at Mount Vernon, with a friend or two about me, than to be attended, at the seat of government, by the officers of state, and the representatives of every power in Europe."[236] He loved being with his family and friends, but he also loved the estate itself. Washington said of Mount Vernon, "No estate in United America is more pleasantly situated than this."[237]

Washington's homes reflected his character, whether his permanent residence at Mount Vernon or temporary homes during the war and while president. At all of these places, there were order, punctuality, and economy. Great productivity flowed from the man and his homes. The decor at Mount Vernon was impressive but not ostentatious. The regular habits of the man and household were plain, yet dignified and correct.

Washington did not just fulfill his duties to his wife, family, mother, and relatives, but he was devoted to them and their well-being and loved them greatly. Nelly Custis said that he was always considerate and tender toward Martha and that there was perfect harmony "between her grandmamma and the general."[238] From the time of his marriage until his death, he always wore a miniature portrait of Martha around his neck. As was noted earlier, he wrote many letters to her, but she destroyed them after he died, per his request.[239] Only three of their letters survived, and each shows his love for her, his character, and his strong faith. He wrote on July 20, 1758, before their marriage and while in the midst of the French and Indian War, to "one whose life is now inseparable from mine. Since that happy hour when we made our pledges to each other, my thoughts have been continually going to you as another Self. That an all-powerful Providence may keep us both in safety is the prayer of your ever faithful and affectionate friend."[240]

After his appointment as commander of the Continental army, he wrote to her on June 18, 1775, explaining how he did not seek the position and did all he could to avoid it, "not only from my unwillingness to part with you and the family, but from a consciousness of its being a trust too great for my capacity." His love and devotion were then expressed quite eloquently: "I should enjoy more real happiness in one month with you at home than

I have the most distant prospect of finding abroad, if my stay were to be seven times seven years." He closed by expressing his reliance on Providence.[241]

Five days after this, he wrote a quick note to her:

My Dearest: As I am within a few minutes of leaving this city, I would not think of departing from it with out dropping you a line, especially as I do not know whether it may be in my power to write again till I get to the camp at Boston. I go fully trusting in that providence, which has been more bountiful to me than I deserve and in full confidence of a happy meeting with you some time in the fall. I have no time to add more as I am surrounded with company to take leave of me. I return an unalterable affection for you which neither time or distance can change.[242]

With her well-being in mind, he wrote to his brother John Augustine: "I shall hope that my Friends will visit and endeavor to keep up the spirits of my Wife as much as they can, as my departure will, I know, be a cutting stroke upon her; and on this account alone, I have many very disagreeable sensations."[243]

Washington respected and listened to his wife and was always kind toward her. A guest at Mount Vernon said that one night, after all had retired to their bedrooms, he heard Martha talking to Washington in a very animated manner about something he had done that she thought should have been done differently. Washington listened silently to all she had to say. When she had finished and grown silent, he spoke, "Now good sleep to you, my dear."[244]

Washington was devoted to Martha's children and grandchildren. When his stepson died during the war, he adopted John Parke Custis's two youngest children as his own. He took his parental responsibilities seriously, as reflected in many letters to them in which he gave instruction in many areas of life. While in Philadelphia as president, he advised Nelly, who at age sixteen was attending her first ball, to govern her passions. "A hint here," he wrote, "men and women feel the same inclinations to each other now that they always have done, . . . and you . . . may find, perhaps, that the passions of your sex are easier raised then allayed. Do not, therefore, boast too soon or too strongly of your insensibility to, or resistance of, its powers. In the composition of the human frame there is a good deal of inflammable matter, however dormant it may lie for a time, and . . . when the torch is put to it, that which is within you may burst into a blaze." He went on to explain that love is more than "involuntary passion," "love may and therefore ought to be under the guidance of reason," and in the future when the time came, reason, not emotions, should be central in deciding who would be her spouse.[245] Four years later, Nelly married Lawrence Lewis, Washington's favorite nephew and the son of his only sister, Elizabeth.

He also took time while president to instruct fifteen-year-old George Washington Parke Custis, who was attending school. Washington wrote that he was glad to hear Custis had been studying diligently and "fulfilling those obligations which are enjoined by your Creator and due to his creatures," for education would help render him "a useful member of society." "You are now extending into that stage of life when good or bad habits are formed. When the mind will be turned to the things useful and praiseworthy, or to dissipation and vice. Fix on whichever it may, it will stick by you; for you know it has been said, and truly, 'that as the twig is bent so it will grow.'" Washington encouraged him to study hard, avoid vice, receive mature advice, but also take time for "manly exercise." He wrote, "True friendship is a plant of slow growth," and thus cautioned him to take time to weigh the character of those he befriended.[246] This and other letters contained much similar fatherly advice.

When necessary, Washington addressed waywardness in his son, including the time Custis committed some "error" while at Princeton. Writing to Washington, Custis expressed deep remorse and sought forgiveness. Washington responded: "If your sorrow and repentance for the disquietude occasioned by the preceding letter, your resolution to abandon the ideas which were therein expressed, are sincere, I shall not only heartily forgive, but will forget also, and bury in oblivion all that has passed."[247] Washington's advice had a great effect upon his son, who wrote: "Your letter . . . is engraven on my mind, and has taken root in a soil which I shall cultivate, and which, I hope, may become fruitful."[248]

Washington cared for his mother throughout his life. While she was quite self-sufficient, managing Ferry Farm on her own for decades after the death of her husband, Washington continued to keep an eye on her and visited her when he could. When she was too old to continue to live on the farm, he procured a home for her in Fredericksburg, where she lived until her death in 1789.

On his way to the first presidential inauguration, Washington stopped in Fredericksburg to visit his mother, "never expecting to see her more."[249] Though no doubt joyful at her son's accomplishments, his great fame had no effect on her simple mode of living. Proud that he had been a good son and done his duty as a man, she gave him a final blessing: "Go, George, fulfill the high destinies which Heaven appears to have intended you for; go, my son, and may that Heaven's and a mother's blessing be with you always."[250] She died about four months later, at the age of eighty-five. After the death of his mother on August 25, 1789, Washington wrote to his sister: "Awful, and affecting as the death of a Parent is, there is consolation in knowing, that Heaven has spared ours to an age, beyond which few attain, and favored her with the full enjoyment of her mental faculties, and as much bodily strength as usually falls to the lot of fourscore. Under these considerations and a hope that she is translated to a happier place, it is the duty of her relatives to yield due submission to the decrees of the Creator."[251]

In her will, his mother clearly revealed her hope for eternity, "recommending my soul in the hands of my Creator, hoping for a remission of all my sins through the merits and mediation of Jesus Christ, the Saviour of mankind."[252]

Washington's devotion to his friends might best be seen in his relationship with Lafayette. The general quickly embraced and trusted this young, freedom-loving, idealistic French nobleman as his own son. Lafayette wrote of Washington: "From the time of my first landing in America, up to the campaign of 1781, I had enjoyed the attachment, nay, parental regards of the matchless chief."[253] To honor the "matchless chief," he named his son George Washington Lafayette. The nobleman was a leader in the French Revolution at its beginning, even sending the key to the Bastille to Washington, but as more extreme revolutionaries seized control of the revolution, Lafayette's life was threatened and he was imprisoned. When this news reached Washington, he did all he could to secure his release, but to no effect. One evening, when discussing Lafayette's fate with a friend, he "became so deeply affected, that his eyes filled with tears, and his whole great soul was stirred to its very depths."[254] George Washington Lafayette, then seventeen or eighteen years old, fled to America in 1797, and at Washington's invitation, he lived at Mount Vernon for about two years.[255]

Washington was loyal to others, and they were loyal to him. He respected others, and he was greatly respected by his family, friends, troops, or colleagues. At age twenty-four, he was given overall command of the Virginia forces raised to protect the frontier. Some men who wanted this position started rumors challenging his abilities. He wrote to friends in the government, saying he would be glad to resign, that he was only burdened by his service, with no benefits, and that he only accepted the position to meet the call of duty. Landon Carter wrote: "How are we grieved to hear Colonel George Washington hinting to his country, that he is willing to retire!" He asked the young colonel to forget "that any thing has been said to your dishonor; and recollect, that it could not have come from any man that knew you." Another friend wrote that he never heard that Washington's conduct was questioned:

"Whenever you are mentioned, it is with the greatest respect." The Speaker of the House responded: "Our hopes, dear George, are all fixed on you for bringing our affairs to a happy issue."[256] These remarks, from older leading men to young Washington, reveal the height of respect he had already obtained.

Washington esteemed others, and he was greatly esteemed by people throughout the world—by both those who knew him only by his great accomplishments and by those who knew him more closely. His friends and family were his greatest admirers, and they wanted nothing more than to be admired by him. G. W. P. Custis wrote: "I will now conclude, with expressing, what I have always had nearest my heart, a desire of your esteem. Be assured naught shall be wanting on my part to obtain the same; and that the great Parent of the universe may prolong your days, is the sincere prayer of your ever affectionate."[257]

Physical Character and Presence

You are the only human being for whom I ever felt an awful reverence.

—Lord Erskine

WASHINGTON WAS A LARGE and powerful man. His nephew, Maj. Lawrence Lewis, asked him what his height was in the prime of life. He replied, "In my best days, Lawrence, I stood six feet and two inches in ordinary shoes."[258] Washington told the governor of Canada in 1799 that "my weight, in my best days, sir, never exceeded from two hundred and ten to twenty."[259] G. W. P. Custis said his physique was unique. Unlike most athletes who are V-shaped from the shoulders down, Washington "descended from the shoulders to the hips in perpendicular lines. . . . His limbs were long, large, and sinewy. . . . His joints, feet, and hands, were large; and, could a cast have been made from his right hand (so far did its dimensions exceed nature's model), it would have been preserved in museums for ages as the anatomical wonder of the eighteenth century."[260]

Washington exhibited great strength and courage from a young age. His strength and athletic skills stayed with him throughout his life. In the battle of the Monongahela, even though weak with sickness, a spectator commented, "I saw him take hold of a brass field-piece as if it had been a stick."[261] As general, he once stopped a fight between two soldiers by grabbing them behind the neck, one in each hand, and knocking their heads together.[262] When he was older, he saw some young men competing to see who could throw a heavy stone the farthest. After observing the measurement of the longest throw, he said, "I think I can beat that," and he tossed a stone well beyond that mark and then quietly walked on.[263]

Thomas Jefferson wrote that his person "was fine, his stature exactly what one would wish, his deportment easy, erect, and noble; the best horseman of his age, and the most graceful figure that could be seen on horseback."[264] Witnessing the general at the battle of Monmouth, Lafayette said, "Never had I beheld so superb a man."[265] Jedidiah Morse remarked: "There was in his whole appearance an unusual dignity and gracefulness which at once secured him profound respect, and cordial esteem. He seemed born to command his fellow men."[266]

Washington was commanding in presence as well as in physical size. Jared Sparks reported that "there was a dignity in his person and manner, not easy to be defined, which impressed every one that saw him for the first time with an instinctive deference and awe."[267] He emanated a presence; as chaplain Ashbel Green noted, "There was more of the indefinable quality called *presence* in President Washington, than any other person I have ever known."[268] His commanding figure may have had something to do with this, but it was mostly his character that produced this presence. An English gentleman added: "There was a commanding air in his appearance which excited respect, and forbade too great a freedom towards him, independently of that species of awe which is always felt in the moral influence of a great character."[269]

Custis observed that "man never was born of woman, who could approach the great Washington, and not feel a degree of awe and veneration from his presence."[270] Elkanah Watson, a visitor to Mount Vernon in 1785, said, "I trembled with awe, as I came into the presence of this great man." But after spending some time in his home, Watson learned what other acquaintances of Washington knew quite well: he was also kind and humble. Watson added: "I found him kind and benignant in the domestic circle; revered and beloved by all around him; agreeably social, without ostentation; delighting in anecdote and adventures; without assumption. . . . He modestly waived all allusions to the events in which he had acted so glorious and conspicuous a part."[271]

A Continental soldier described well both the external and internal characteristics of the general:

George Washington of Virginia! . . . Who has not heard of his wisdom, his noble spirit, his modesty; of his coat torn to rags by bullets in the French and Indian wars? I feared it was like the talk we have heard on the King's birthday, and was prepared for disappointment. But he has conquered me. I am like a man thrown and stunned, who is trying to think how it happened.

He is a big man . . . Yet . . . this is the smallest part of him. . . . I wondered why I felt a kind of awe in his presence; but I know now.

The big thing is inside of him; it reaches out and touches you when you look in his eyes and when he moves his hands. It hits you again when you hear his voice. There are three words that come to me as I think of him; they are: Power, Vitality and Kindness. I think that he has a mind as strong as our best pair of oxen, and that God is driving it. He said little. . . . He has a good-natured face, a bit weathered, with a pock-mark here and there—not handsome. . . . [W]hen he stood up, straight as an arrow, and smiled at us, he was magnificent; it's a big word, nor carelessly chosen. He wore his riding boots. His blue and buff uniform with golden epaulettes and buttons was spotless and well fitted. From shoe to ruffles every detail in his dress was admirable. Still it was not his look or his manners, genteel as they were, that reduced me to a sense of smallness. It was the man under it all. . . . He has doubled my faith in our cause and in our ultimate victory.[272]

At first thought, Washington's speech would not seem to be like his presence, for it was not imposing like his physical person. He was not known for his oratory, he did not speak often on the floor of the legislature, and he did not deliver pithy lines with burning passion that swayed men to action. Silas Deane wrote of Washington at the First Continental Congress that "he speaks very modestly and in cool but determined style and accent."[273] However, upon closer examination, his words often carried a great power that awed those who heard them. They carried a great force. William Johnson described one such incident:

> So far back as 1756 we find him endeavoring to impress upon the soldiers under his command a profound reverence for the name and the majesty of God, and repeatedly, in his public orders during the Revolution, the inexcusable offense of profaneness was rebuked.
>
> On a certain occasion he had invited a number of officers to dine with him. While at table one of them uttered an oath. General Washington dropped his knife and fork in a moment, and in his deep undertone, and characteristic dignity and deliberation, said, "I thought that we all supposed ourselves gentlemen." He then resumed his knife and fork and went on as before. The remark struck like an electric shock, and, as was intended, did execution, as his observations in such cases were apt to do. No person swore at the table after that. When dinner was over, the officer referred to said to a companion that if the General had given him a blow over the head with his sword, he could have borne it, but that the home thrust which he received was too much—it was too much for a gentleman![274]

The value and force of words depends upon who stands behind them; that is, upon the nature of him who utters them. Washington's character and presence made his words powerful.

Industry and Diligence

*When we consider the volume of his official
papers . . . we are scarcely able to believe that the
space of one man's life should have
comprehended the doing of so many things, and
doing them so well.*

—G. W. P. Custis

ABITUAL DILIGENCE OR STEADY attention to
the business at hand—that is, industry—is
an essential characteristic of a good leader. From his
youth, Washington learned to be excellent in all his work
and actions. His early notebooks were neat and precise
and reflect an excellent spirit, even using great care when
correcting a mistake. Likewise, his later records of business transactions are detailed and precise. His voluminous
writings touch on a vast range of subjects, and the sheer
quantity reveals his diligence. His grooming and appearance showed his great taste and sense of order, and he
was always seen in the proper attire. This was also true at
home, where even his relatives rarely saw him not properly dressed.

His home, horses, and equipage show his excellence as well. People who saw him ride through the streets of Philadelphia noted his immaculate dress, but they also saw "that his horse's hoofs were blackened and polished as thoroughly as his own boots."[275]

Washington showed this kind of attention to all such small details throughout his life. He described items of his household in minute detail and calculated precisely the materials needed for his farms. This was true even while he was weighed down with the great concerns of the nation. He was never above small affairs. He enjoyed planting trees and shrubs with his own hands at Mount Vernon. He walked through the woods and selected young trees to be transplanted to preselected spots in accordance with his own detailed plan to make his lawn and home pleasant and beautiful.

Throughout the war and during his presidential years, he stayed up to date with the affairs of his farms. His manager, Lund Washington, wrote to him two or three times a month, conveying detailed information on what was happening at Mount Vernon. Washington trusted Lund to make the necessary decisions to maintain the property, but his own industry and sense of responsibility can be seen in his letters to Lund, regularly giving specific instructions on the overall running of the plantation—planting, crop sales, and such—but also paying great attention to small details. And he managed to do this while commanding an army at war, while forming a new government, and while governing a new nation!

The volume and extent of his correspondence during the Revolutionary War is a great testament to Washington's industry and ability to manage many different things simultaneously. He wrote hundreds of letters to Congress, informing the legislators of everything he was doing; he wrote to various state leaders to solicit their support and approval; and he wrote to local leaders. At the same time, he maintained a voluminous personal correspondence with his wife, relatives, friends, and his farm manager. About twenty-five of the thirty-seven volumes of his writings (as edited by John C. Fitzpatrick) cover the war period from 1775 to 1783. Yet these are not all of his letters, since his correspondence with his wife was destroyed after his death and other letters have been discovered since Fitzpatrick's compilation. While his aides assisted in writing and copying some of his letters, each epistle expressed his ideas. Though he dictated most of these letters, he also wrote many with his own hand. He sanctioned every idea in every communication that bore his name. This massive correspondence was produced while organizing, training, and equipping an army not accustomed to military discipline and in the face of a superior enemy.

Washington's daily routine reflects his sense of industry. While at home, he awoke early every morning and spent a few hours in his library, reading and writing. He also took time each evening for writing, even when he was in the field with the army and during his presidency. In addition, he often wrote letters during the day. G. W. P. Custis commented: "When we consider the volume of his official papers—his vast foreign, public, and private correspondence—we are scarcely able to believe that the space of one man's life should have comprehended the doing of so many things, and doing them so well."[276]

Washington ultimately succeeded at many things in his life due to his never-yielding perseverance. He never quit, even in the worst of situations, which was more important in winning the Revolutionary War than any skills he possessed as a general.

He was punctual and organized. Throughout his life, he awakened every morning around four o'clock and retired every night around nine o'clock. He was punctual for meals, for meetings, in his correspondence, and in managing his affairs at home and in public service. To a theater manager who said he would delay raising the curtain if need be, until Washington arrived, the president replied, "I will be punctual, sir, to the time; nobody waits a single moment for me."[277] And he demanded that those around him be punctual as well. Anyone who visited the president, arrived and departed at the scheduled time, knowing "the president is punctual." His organizational skill was such that during his visit to the southern states in the spring of 1791, in which he traveled nineteen hundred miles in about three months, the only time he departed from his itinerary was due to high waters or excessively bad roads.

One of the central reasons for Washington's greatness was his diligence. In all he set his hand to do, both small and great, he was completely devoted to accomplishing the task at hand with the greatest excellence. It is seen in his copybooks, in the responsibilities he assumed when his father died, in his excellent work as a surveyor, in his leadership as an envoy for the Virginia governor, and in fulfilling his duties in the state militia. He was an excellent farmer, expanding and developing his estate throughout his life. He served with distinction as a leader in the Virginia legislature as well as on his church vestry. His thoroughness and industry in his early life enabled him to take on the greater tasks of leading the colonies to independence and in establishing a constitutional republic. All of the experiences of his maturing years served as a training ground in which he developed the traits necessary for the high callings of his life. He was diligent in little things, and thus able to lead many in the large affairs that loomed over his state and his country. He was diligent in all his business affairs, standing later in the forefront of the leading men of the nation and becoming the father of his nation.

COMPASSION AND EMPATHY

I feel superabundantly for them, and, from my
soul, I pity those miseries, which it is neither in
my power to relieve nor prevent.

WASHINGTON WAS A STRONG, forceful man who pushed through any obstacles, yet he was also kind and tenderhearted, showing great compassion for others. He was secure in himself and had no fear of displaying emotions at times, as when he wept at the death of his stepdaughter. As a young man, his tender emotions were revealed in some of his love verses and remarks in regard to meeting young ladies. As he grew older, his duty required him to put the public good above emotional expression, but he still showed much empathy toward others, as when he adopted his grandchildren at the death of his stepson.

As the young commander of the Virginia forces tasked with protecting the western settlements from Indian raids during the French and Indian War, Washington was greatly affected by the plight of the settlers, who, he wrote, "are really frightened out of their senses."[278] He was heartbroken at his inability to do much for them. In a letter to Robert Dinwiddie seeking more assistance, Washington lamented being induced to accept the job, feeling completely helpless to relieve the anguish of so many families. He saw that many would blame him for the sufferings by not driving away the Indians. His empathy and compassionate heart are apparent in his words: "The supplicating tears of the women and moving petitions of the men, melt me into such deadly sorrow, that I solemnly declare, if I know my own mind, I could offer myself a willing sacrifice to the butchering enemy, provided that would contribute to the people's ease."[279]

After the battle of Trenton in December 1776, hundreds of Hessians were taken prisoner. As they were marched through Pennsylvania, many people harassed these non-English-speaking mercenaries, looking at them as despicable professional soldiers. But Washington placed notices throughout the countryside saying that these men were not to blame for the war; they had been forced to fight by their sovereign who had sold them to Great Britain. After this news was disseminated, the Hessians were treated with much more respect.

Washington's concern for his troops can be seen in his words and actions during the winter at Valley Forge. His letters seeking aid to relieve their distressed situation flow with empathy and compassion—"I feel superabundantly for them, and, from my soul, I pity those miseries, which it is neither in my power to relieve nor prevent."[280]

Many visited Washington at Mount Vernon, and all were treated with the utmost respect. Because he was more famous than the kings of Europe and greatly revered by so many, visitors often approached him with awe. Elkanah Watson described his January 1785 visit to Mount Vernon: "I had feasted my imagination for several days in the near prospect of a visit to Mount Vernon, the seat of Washington. No pilgrim ever approached Mecca with deeper enthusiasm." Even though he had letters of introduction from Gen. Nathanael Greene and another friend of Washington, he noted, "I trembled with awe as I came into the presence of this great man." He was cordially received, and Washington "soon put me at ease by unbending in a free and affable conversation. . . . I observed a peculiarity in his smile, which seemed to illuminate his eye; his whole countenance beamed with intelligence, while it commanded confidence and respect." At the time, Watson had a bad cold and cough, and Washington recommended some remedies, which he declined. When Watson went to bed for the night, his coughing increased. After a little time, "the door of my room was gently opened, and on drawing my bed-curtains, to my utter astonishment, I beheld Washington himself, standing at my bedside, with a bowl of hot tea in his hand. I was mortified and distressed beyond expression." He commented that this kindness and compassion of the general only increased his awe for the man. Watson said of his two-day visit, "To have communed with such a man in the bosom of his family, I shall always regard as one of the highest privileges, and most cherished incidents of my life."[281]

Washington's concern for others above himself remained until the end. While on his deathbed, he regretted being a burden to his wife, doctors, and secretary. He even motioned for a servant who had been standing for some time to take a seat.

HUMILITY AND MODESTY

*Humility and a pacific temper of mind, . . . were
the characteristics of the Divine Author of our
blessed religion; . . . without an humble imitation
of whose example in these things, we can never
hope to be a happy nation.*

*H*UMILITY IS A DIFFICULT quality to find in those
who are rich and famous and powerful. In
his later years, Washington was certainly the most famous
and powerful person in America, and he was one of the
richest, yet he was also a modest and humble individual.
He learned humility and modesty from his parents, and
these qualities were reinforced throughout his life. He drew
little attention to the hardships and sacrifices he endured.

His modesty became apparent at an early age. When
he contracted smallpox while in Barbados with his
brother in 1751, he barely mentioned the agonizing ordeal in his diary, though he was extremely ill for three
weeks.[282] His entries show no hint of self-pity or expression of self-concern, and this remained true throughout
his life. What is evident are many examples of his concern
for others and desire to help.

Washington was first elected to the House of Burgesses in 1758 and took office just after his marriage in 1759. During his introduction, Speaker John Robinson thanked the colonel for his years of military service and enumerated his accomplishments in glowing words. The Speaker paused to allow Washington to reply. Never known for his oratorical skills, coupled with embarrassment at the high praise, the words died on his lips. "He blushed, stammered, and trembled, for a second," when Robinson, a friend who was aware of Washington's modesty, said, "Sit down, Mr. Washington; your modesty is equal to your valour; and that surpasses the power of any language that I possess."[283]

In June 1775, after the delegates of the Second Continental Congress were called to order, John Adams proposed that the army at Boston be taken over by the Congress and that a general be named to command it. There was one among them whom he had in mind, one "very well known to all of us; a gentleman, whose skill and experience as an officer, whose independent fortune, great talents, and excellent universal character would command the approbation of all America, and unite the cordial exertion of all the colonies better than any other person in the Union."[284] Adams, knowing that John Hancock fancied himself as the man for this command, thought he saw a look of anticipation on Hancock's face as he spoke. But when Hancock learned that Adams was speaking of a Virginian, his face fell.[285] There was a much different reaction from Washington, who had no ambitions for the position. Adams recalled: "Mr. Washington, who happened to sit near the door, as soon as he heard me allude to him, from his usual modesty, darted into the library-room."[286]

After Washington was unanimously elected on June 15 as commander in chief, Adams wrote to his wife, Abigail, on June 17, "The Congress have made Choice of the modest and virtuous, the amiable, generous and brave George Washington Esqr., to be the General of the American Army. . . . This Appointment will have a great Effect, in cementing and securing the Union of these Colonies."[287]

Washington did not believe he was qualified to fulfill the role of commanding general, but with his determined humility, he was willing to respond to the call of duty. His motives in accepting the command were not for personal gain but rather for humble service to his country and the cause of liberty, because he refused any salary, requesting only that his expenses would be covered.[288]

If any were to think that Washington was just saying these things to maintain a public image, they should note that he communicated the same ideas in private. In a letter to Martha explaining his appointment as commander in chief and saying he had to depart immediately to Boston, he added that he had not sought the appointment but "used every endeavor in my power to avoid it. . . . It was utterly out of my power to refuse this appointment, without exposing my character to such censures, as would have reflected dishonor upon myself, and given pain to my friends."[289]

He expressed similar ideas to his stepson, John Parke Custis,[290] and to his brother-in-law, Burwell Bassett, to whom he affirmed "the Justice of our Cause" and added: "May God grant, therefore, that my acceptance of it, may be attended with some good to the common cause, and without Injury (from want of knowledge) to my own reputation."[291]

To his brother John Augustine, he wrote of the perils ahead: "I am now to bid adieu to you, and to every kind of domestick ease, for a while. I am Imbarked on a wide Ocean, boundless in its prospect, and from whence, perhaps, no safe harbour is to be found. I have been called upon by the unanimous Voice of the Colonies to take the Command of the Continental Army. An honour I neither sought after, nor desired, as I am thoroughly convinced, that it requires great Abilities, and much more experience, than I am Master of."[292]

Washington's humility was also apparent in his response to the officers who proposed making him king and his becoming the American Cincinnatus by eagerly walking away from power at the close of the war to return to his life as a farmer. Washington's modesty was also apparent when people looked at him. Abigail Adams described the first time she saw him: "Dignity, ease and complacency, the gentleman and the soldier, look agreeably blended in him. Modesty marks every line and feature of his face."[293]

Washington did not seek recognition and tried to avoid when possible the accolades of the people. When the capital moved from New York to Philadelphia in 1790, he planned to slip off unobserved, but he was closely watched. On the day of departure, with his baggage loaded, he arose before dawn to leave. G. W. P. Custis recalled: "The lights were yet burning, when the president came into the room where his family were assembled, evidently much pleased in the belief that all was right, when, immediately under the windows, the band of the artillery struck up Washington's March. 'There!' he exclaimed, 'it's all over; we are found out. Well, well, they must have their own way."[294] A great celebration ensued in New York and all along the route to Philadelphia.

People loved him so much, John Adams feared they were making a god out of him. Biographer Caroline M. Kirkland recorded: "So great was the general reverence expressed for Washington, that a little boy walking with his father in the streets of Philadelphia, and meeting the general, exclaimed—'Why, father! General Washington is only a man, after all!' Washington looked at him thoughtfully, and said—'That's all, my little fellow, that's all!'"[295]

His humility stands even brighter when viewed in light of the unparalleled praise he received. Many did see him as a god or savior, and one charge of the cabal to replace him during the war was that people were making a god of him. And after the victories at Trenton and Princeton, he was regarded with wonder by all nations. They applauded his character and saw him as the savior of his country.[296] His birthday began to be celebrated in 1784 and continued throughout his life and well beyond. During his trips to the states during his presidency, massive crowds greeted him wherever he went. His humble response to these things reflected his greatness.

Washington did not speak about himself or any of his accomplishments. His adopted daughter, Nelly Custis, who lived in his house for twenty years, recalled: "He was a silent, thoughtful man. He spoke little generally; never of himself. I never heard him relate a single act of his during the war."[297] Jared Sparks noted that Washington was "without vanity, ostentation, or pride, he never spoke of himself or his actions, unless required by circumstances which concerned the public interests."[298] While in Washington's company, Bishop William White pondered, "If a stranger to his person were present, he would never have known from anything said by the President that he was conscious of having distinguished himself in the eye of the world."[299]

Honesty

*Honesty in States, as well as in individuals, will
ever be found the soundest policy.*

THE NAME OF WASHINGTON has been associated
with telling the truth for generations. Every
American of earlier times would have matched, "I cannot
tell a lie," with Washington's name. This is no longer true,
however, due primarily to the changing philosophical foundation of American education. History is now taught from
an evolutionary perspective, with an emphasis on socio-
economic factors; thus, few are introduced to the character of the man who for two centuries was known as the
Father of the Country. In addition, the concept of truth is
no longer taught, because truth is viewed as relative.
There is no absolute truth, because what is true for one
person, may not be true for another. All people and all
truths are tolerated—except for those who believe there is
a standard and source of absolute truth.

Washington and the Founding Fathers would consider the modern assault on truth to be foolish, the product of ignorant men whose ideas would lead to the internal overthrow of the free republic. Honesty—a disposition to conform to correct moral principles or truth—is an essential quality for the citizens of any nation seeking to live in liberty. Washington considered being known as an honest man to be the highest honor he could obtain. On August 28, 1788, he wrote to Alexander Hamilton: "Still I hope I shall always possess firmness and virtue enough to maintain (what I consider the most enviable of all titles) the character of *an honest man.*"[300]

Washington was raised by his parents to tell the truth. A reverent fear of God, backed by his parents' firm discipline, helped to implant within him a strong conviction to be honest. There are many anecdotal stories from Washington's youth that depict the noble honesty of the boy. The most famous was first recorded by Mason Weems.

Weems had been the minister at Washington's parish church, and he wrote a popular book on the general's life. Two brief editions were published before Washington's death; other editions followed. The 1806 fifth edition contained the cherry tree, the cabbage seed, and other stories that made the book famous. Many of these stories were retold by others. William Holmes McGuffey included some in his famous readers, which helped to cement these stories into American lore. While some historians view aspects of Weems's writings as fable, showing how some stories are inaccurate and how others have no collaborating evidence, Weems's personal knowledge of Washington and his family gave him insight into the man such that we should not summarily discount all he wrote.

Weems was the first to tell the story of Washington's chopping down the cherry tree with his hatchet and the subsequent honesty of the boy in response to his father's question: "I can't tell a lie, Pa; you know I can't tell a lie. I did cut it with my hatchet." Augustine Washington's response shows the high regard early Americans had for truth: "Run to my arms, you dearest boy, . . . run to my arms; glad am I, George, that you killed my tree; for you have paid me for it a thousand fold. Such an act of heroism in my son is more worth than a thousand trees, though blossomed with silver, and their fruits of purest gold."[301]

While the specifics of this incident are in doubt, there is no doubt of Washington's love of truth or of his courage, which were displayed throughout his life. His parents most certainly instilled these traits within their son. His father would have used the events of Washington's youthful life to teach these important principles. Therefore, there could easily be much truth in the many anecdotal stories recorded by Weems and others.

Washington's family and friends related similar incidences. G. W. P. Custis wrote of a high-spirited ungovernable horse, Mary Washington's favorite, that resisted all attempts "to subject him to the rein." No man had been able to ride this vicious horse. One day Washington told his young friends he would ride the horse if they helped him catch and bridle it. After doing so, he leaped on the horse, and the animal responded in great fury. The struggle was so terrific his friends feared for his safety, but he "clung to the furious steed." The conflict was long, but the rider was gaining control, when eventually "the gallant horse, summoning all his powers to one mighty effort, reared, and plunged with tremendous violence, burst his noble heart, and died in an instant." The rider was "alive, unharmed, and without a wound."

Shortly after, at the morning meal, Washington's mother asked about her horses, especially her favorite. When she noticed some embarrassment from the boys, she asked again. Washington replied, "Your favorite, the sorrel, is dead, madam." He then told her what had happened. She responded: "It is well; but while I regret the loss of my favorite, I rejoice in my son, who always speaks the truth."[302]

Regardless of whether these stories are true or not, they reflect the training and character of the man. They have also been used to communicate a love of truth to millions of Americans.

Washington displayed honesty and integrity throughout his life—in his open dealings with state officials during the French and Indian War, in how he conducted his business affairs, gaining a reputation for excellence and honesty even in foreign ports, in handling the many difficult situations during the Revolutionary War, and in responding to the call of his nation to serve two terms as president. He was upright and incorruptible in all his actions and affairs.

Washington's straightforward honesty helped to diffuse the Conway cabal during the war. Gen. Thomas Conway and others had suggested to some congressmen that Washington should be replaced as commanding general. Responding to Henry Laurens, the president of the Congress, regarding the faction against him, Washington commented that this caused him some personal pain, but of more concern to him were "the dangerous consequences . . . to the common cause." As his desire was to promote the public good, he wrote, "I would not desire in the least degree to suppress a free spirit of enquiry into any part of my conduct." He said he was not above fault: "Why should I expect to be exempt from censure; the unfailing lot of an elevated station? Merit and talents, with which I can have no pretensions of rivalship, have ever been subject to it. My heart tells me it has been my unremitted aim to do the best circumstances would permit; yet, I may have been very often mistaken in my judgment of the means, and may, in many instances deserve the imputation of error."[303]

His well-known integrity pushed aside the baseless charges of the cabal. Conway came to see his error and wrote to Washington, repenting of his conduct. "My career will soon be over," he wrote, "therefore justice and truth prompt me to declare my last sentiments. You are in my eyes the great and good man."[304]

During the height of the friction, Lafayette wrote to von Steuben concerning Washington: "His honesty, his frankness, his sensibility, his virtue, to the full extent in which this word can be understood, are above all praise."[305]

CHARITY AND PHILANTHROPY

I believe, that man was not designed by the All-wise Creator, to live for himself alone.

*W*ASHINGTON WAS GENEROUS THROUGHOUT his life. He showed his faith by his works, as the apostle James describes true faith (James 1:2–27). Washington donated to many charities and needy individuals and instructed those in his charge to be charitable as well. To his adopted son, he wrote: "Never let an indigent person ask, without receiving something, if you have the means; always recollecting in what light the widow's mite was viewed."[306]

He wrote Lund Washington on November 26, 1775: "Let the Hospitality of the House, with respect to the poor, be kept up; Let no one go hungry away. If any of these kind of People should be in want of Corn, supply their necessities, provided it does not encourage them in idleness; and I have no objection to your giving my Money in Charity, to the Amount of forty or fifty Pounds a Year. . . . What I mean, by having no objection, is, that it is my desire that it should be done." While generous, he was also responsible, as noted above where he did not want to encourage idleness. He went on to say to Lund that he had "no doubts, of your observing the greatest economy and frugality." He reminded him "that I do not get a farthing for my services here more than my Expenses; It becomes necessary, therefore, for me to be saving at home."[307]

One of his managers after the war said: "I had orders from Gen. Washington to fill a corn-house every year, for the sole use of the poor in my neighbourhood, to whom it was a most seasonable and precious relief, saving numbers of poor women and children from extreme want, and blessing them with plenty."[308]

In considering ways to provide for the poor, Washington also applied biblical principles of gleaning, which requires labor from those who are able to work. He had a number of fishing stations on the Potomac River next to his farms as part of his business activities. One was made available to the poor and was equipped with the necessary equipment to hook herring and other fish. Honest and industrious poor people could use this facility for no charge and at any time simply by applying to Washington's overseer. Washington even ordered his workers to assist anyone who needed help in bringing in their catch. Thus, any poor people in the area around Mount Vernon could obtain food for themselves and their families.[309]

Washington gave to the poor, to the church, to schools and colleges, to individuals, to religious societies, and to the community. He generously supported both Pohick and Christ Churches. He gave fifty pounds per year for the education of poor children in Alexandria, and in his will, he left four thousand dollars for the same purpose.[310] He endowed Liberty Hall Academy (present-day Washington and Lee University) with ten thousand dollars, assuring its continuance.[311] He gave shares of stock to help establish a university in the District of Columbia, and he offered to pay the expenses of at least two or three students to attend the university.[312] Since he kept private such acts of charity, it is likely similar kindnesses were done at other times. He supported efforts to Christianize the Indians and offered his own western lands as a place for missionaries and industrious immigrants to establish settlements that would be examples to introduce the Indians to civilization and Christian principles.[313]

Washington also showed his generosity by welcoming myriads of friends and well-wishers to his home, hosting them at great expense. Even before his great fame, he entertained many people almost every day at Mount Vernon. He wrote in his diary in 1768: "Would any person believe that, with a hundred and one cows actually reported at a late enumeration of the cattle, I should still be obliged to buy butter for my family?"[314]

Over the years, many thousands of guests visited Mount Vernon. In one year alone, Washington recorded having nearly one thousand overnight guests. His home was as busy as an inn. Yet he always received these strangers and friends with great kindness and generosity.

While Washington was very generous throughout his life, he was also prudent in his spending. He was especially frugal when handling other people's money, whether that of his stepchildren or taxpayers. He wisely oversaw the inheritances of Martha's children, and as president, he chose a modest home in which to live in Philadelphia, one he could afford.

Washington was very fond of fish, but he did not let his love of fish overcome his prudence. In Philadelphia, Washington's steward, Sam Fraunces, purchased the only shad that was caught in the Delaware River that month. It was very expensive, but he wanted to please the president with this delicacy of which he was so fond, even though orders had been given to set a modest table. When dinner was served, Washington asked about the fish and learned it was the first of the season. Then he asked the price. Fraunces stammered out that it had cost three dollars. "Take it away," thundered the chief. "Take it away, sir; it shall never be said that my table sets such an example of luxury and extravagance."[315]

Unlike most influential military leaders in history, Washington had no taste for war and fought only in self-defense and to advance the cause of liberty. He saw that acts of charity were grander than any acts of conquest. He wrote in 1788 to the Reverend John Lathrop, secretary of the Humane Society in Boston: "How pitiful, in the eye of reason and religion, is that false ambition which desolates the world with fire and sword for the purposes of conquest and fame; when compared to the milder virtues of making our neighbors and our fellow-men as happy as their frail conditions and perishable natures will permit them to be."[316]

Washington's charity not only flowed to the needy and poor, but expressed itself in numerous acts of kindness, both great and small. One anecdote revealing his concern for others was recorded by Washington Irving: "While the army was encamped at Morristown, he one day attended a religious meeting where divine service was to be celebrated in the open air. A chair had been set out for his use. Just before the service commenced, a woman bearing a child in her arms approached. All the seats were occupied. Washington immediately rose, placed her in the chair which had been assigned to him, and remained standing during the whole service."[317]

Washington's entire life was one of giving—giving of his time, his talents, his money, his private life, his immense energy. He gave his country forty years of service, most without remuneration. He gave to his family, friends, strangers, and the poor. To all these, he gave cheerfully with no thought of return.

WISDOM AND SOUND JUDGMENT

*To secure the blessings which a gracious
Providence has placed within our reach, will call
for the cool and deliberate exertion of patriotism,
firmness, and wisdom.*

WASHINGTON WAS PRUDENT, WISE, and just.
Thomas Jefferson recalled:

His mind was great and powerful, without being of the
very first order; his penetration strong, . . . and as far as
he saw, no judgment was ever sounder. It was slow in
operation, being little aided by invention or imagination,
but sure in conclusion. Hence the common remark of his
officers, of the advantage he derived from councils of war,
where hearing all suggestions, he selected whatever was
best; and certainly no general ever planned his battles
more judiciously. . . . Perhaps the strongest feature in his
character was prudence, never acting until every circumstance, every consideration was maturely weighed; re-
fraining if he saw a doubt, but, when once decided, going
through with his purpose whatever obstacles opposed.[318]

Washington's parents played a large part in developing his sound judgment. Augustine Washington used every opportunity to teach his son how to discern that which was best, most just, and most proper. Washington's exercise of sound judgment in avoiding evil and attempting to do good was reinforced by others who aided his education. His wisdom can be seen in the quality of people he chose to be around, both friends and staff, by his arguments for where to build the new Pohick Church,[319] by the detailed plan he submitted to Congress during the war on the reorganization of the army,[320] by the military decisions he made, and by the way he governed.

Washington recognized British propaganda and did what he could to counteract it. While attending the First Continental Congress in the fall of 1774, he received a letter from Capt. Robert Mackenzie, an old army friend he had known during the French and Indian War, who was then serving in the British army in Boston. Mackenzie mentioned the rebellious conduct of the Bostonians, the great problems they were causing, and their plan to arm themselves for the ultimate goal of independence. Washington replied: "Although you are taught to believe, that the people of Massachusetts are rebellious, setting up for independency, . . . you are abused, grossly abused." He explained how he had talked with the leaders from Massachusetts and knew their "real sentiments," unlike the British leaders "whose business it is, not to disclose truths, but to misrepresent facts in order to justify as much as possible to the world their own conduct." He added that it was not the wish of the government in Massachusetts or in any colony "to set up for independence," which was true at this point. A declaration for independence only came with great reluctance two years later, when no other action was possible. (King George had been fighting with them for fourteen months and declared them rebels and out of his protection, thus it was necessary for them to establish some form of governance.) While there was no thought of independence, Washington told Mackenzie he could be sure "that none of them will ever submit to the loss of those valuable rights and privileges, which are essential to the happiness of every free state, and without which, life, liberty, and property are rendered totally insecure."[321] Similar propaganda flows today from many sources. Leaders and citizens with the discernment of Washington are needed to recognize the truth and stand up to support valuable rights and liberties.

Washington's actions as a legislator reveal that prudence and wisdom were his primary means of influence, as opposed to his speaking skills. G. W. P. Custis wrote, "He might be termed rather a silent than a speaking member of the house of burgesses, although he sometimes addressed the chair, and was listened to with attention and respect, while the excellence of his judgment was put in requisition on all committees."[322] This was also true when he served at the First Continental Congress. He did not enter into public debates, but he proved to be an excellent counselor, one "of solid information and sound judgment."[323]

Some people have criticized Washington for making some bad decisions during the war, for example, tactical maneuvers during the battle of Long Island and failure to evacuate Fort Washington (although the problems here arose from decisions of other commanders). While other generals in history have had more knowledge of military affairs and been better tacticians, it is doubtful if anyone could have done a better job as the commander of American forces in the Revolutionary War. Washington made bold, aggressive moves when necessary (at Dorchester Heights, Trenton, and Princeton), he was cautious when the situation warranted this (at the siege of Boston), he planned and executed brilliant defensive moves (the retreats from Long Island and from Trenton), and he fled from superior numbers to stay alive and fight another day (retreating through New Jersey). He ultimately triumphed, skillfully using all the resources at his disposal (at Yorktown). Some at times criticized his prudent action, but they did not know the great weakness of his army, and he could not make this known for fear the enemy would attack, and any aggressive action would have been met with complete failure. While hindsight may show Washington could have done some things better, there is no doubt his overall strategy and skill brought about victory. A less secure, less wise man could never have achieved the same results. There was no man better suited in all America to be commander in chief at the time of the Revolution.

His wisdom and sound judgment are seen in his sense of justice, exemplified in how he treated captives during the war. The British treated American captives as traitors and rebels, not as captured enemy combatants, and so prisoners received harsh treatment at times. Washington did not retaliate and treat British captives in kind.[324]

His governmental appointments while president reflect his wisdom and good judgment. The first members of the Supreme Court, including Chief Justice John Jay (who would later serve as president of the American Bible Society), were godly men with a biblical view of the law. Washington's cabinet members were men of great knowledge and character, but many held opposing views, which at times erupted in strong disagreements. Washington's ability to manage the conflicts of Thomas Jefferson and Alexander Hamilton, while drawing on their strengths, reflected his great skill.

A final example of his justice occurred during the war, when some people took advantage of the greatly depreciated value of Continental currency by paying their debts with the almost worthless money. Washington spoke out strongly against this, saying, "No honest man would attempt to pay twenty shillings with one."[325] A prominent man in Morristown had used this devalued money to pay a debt, and Washington learned of it. When the man was later introduced to Washington at his headquarters, the general paid little attention to him whereas previously he had been quite cordial to the man. When this happened a second time, Lafayette noticed Washington's uncharacteristic behavior and said, "General, this man seems to be much devoted to you, and yet you have scarcely noticed him." Washington replied with a smile, "I know I have not been cordial; I tried hard to be civil, and attempted to speak to him several times, but that Continental money stopped my mouth."[326]

HUMOR AND ENJOYMENT OF LIFE

*I am now enjoying domestic ease, under the
shadow of my own vine and my own fig-tree.*

*W*ASHINGTON WAS A SERIOUS individual who
performed every duty and sacrificed
much in doing so, but he also greatly enjoyed life, people,
and his own sense of calling. This was especially evident
during his years as a planter before the war, when he entertained often and participated in foxhunts, dances, card
games, games with children, and exhibitions of strength
and athleticism. While he was not wasteful in setting his
table, he entertained quite a number of people. He was
not ostentatious, but he had nice furnishings, rode in an
expensive carriage, and had many fine horses. His dress
was simple and very neat and proper. Later, as president,
he enjoyed the theater "and attended five or six times in
a season."[327]

Between 1759 and 1774, when his farmwork allowed, Washington spent much time foxhunting. This

sport required boldness, athleticism, and equestrian skill, and so the pastime fit him well. He had many horses and hounds to use for such hunts, and guests would come for days to participate in these events. After the Revolutionary War, Washington hunted some, but his enjoyment of agricultural improvements and his many guests caused him to break up his kennel in 1785 and end the pleasures of the chase.[328]

While serious in his deportment, Washington enjoyed good conversation and was known to laugh and be humorous. There are numerous testimonies of his laughing out loud, even as a general in the field. Some of his writings reflect his dry wit, and at times he could be sarcastic. Responding to some who thought he should take more action with the troops at Valley Forge, he wrote: "We find gentlemen, without knowing whether the army was really going into winter quarters or not, reprobating the measure as much as if they thought the soldiers were made of stocks or stones, and equally insensible of frost and snow."[329]

At times Washington displayed a lightheartedness in the midst of great difficulties. During the battle of Monmouth, he observed from a distance some of the officers' valets ride to a small hill, within range of the enemy, and halt to observe through a telescope the actions in the field. The general pointed them out to his officers and remarked, "See those fellows collecting on yonder heights; the enemy will fire on them to a certainty." The British did observe them and, thinking they were officers, fired a 6-pounder at them, which knocked limbs off a tree just behind them. The corps quickly rode off in confusion, which "caused even the countenance of the general-in-chief to relax into a smile."[330]

Another example of light humor in the midst of the difficulties of war can be seen in an August 16, 1779, letter to Dr. John Cochran explaining the humble fare that he and two ladies, whom he had invited to dinner the next day, could expect:

> Since our arrival at this happy spot, we have had a Ham (sometimes a shoulder) of Bacon, to grace the head of the table; a piece of roast Beef adorns the foot; and, a small dish of Greens or Beans (almost imperceptable) decorates the center.
>
> When the Cook has a mind to cut a figure (and this I presume he will attempt to do to morrow) we have two Beefstake-Pyes, or dishes of Crabs in addition, one on each side the center dish, dividing the space, and reducing the distance between dish and dish to about Six feet, which without them, would be near twelve a part. Of late, he has had the surprizing segacity to discover, that apples will make pyes; and it's a question if, amidst the violence of his efforts, we do not get one of apples instead of having both of Beef.
>
> If the ladies can put up with such entertainment, and will submit to partake of it on plates, once tin but now Iron; (not become so by the labor of scowering) I shall be happy to see them. I am, etc.[331]

During the Constitutional Convention, a delegate proposed limiting the standing army to five thousand men. Washington said he would have no disagreement with this if they would amend the proposal to include that no invading enemy could have more than three thousand men.[332]

As was noted earlier, Washington was always punctual at home as well as in his public duties. His public dinners while president always began on time. After waiting for five minutes for differences in timepieces, dinner started. At one dinner, when some congressmen were quite late, Washington, in a pleasant mood, said, "Gentlemen, I have a cook, who never asks whether the company has come, but whether the hour has come."[333]

His lightheartedness can be seen in his diary entry for July 3, 1791, while at York, Pennsylvania: "There being no Episcopal Minister resident in the place, I went to hear morning Service performed in the Dutch reformed Church—which, being in that language not a word of which I understood I was in no danger of becoming a proselyte to its religion by the eloquence of the Preacher."[334]

One day, Washington's land agent, who was also a relative, learned about some land that belonged to Washington that the agent had not known about previously. When they were ending a conversation about this, the agent "remarked, in a jocular tone, that I had had a somewhat singular dream about that land, a few nights before. He asked me what it was. I replied, that I had dreamed he had made me a present of the tract. He smiled, and observed that my dreaming knack was a very convenient one, but why did I not dream at once that he had given me Mount Vernon?"[335]

A few days after this, Washington gave the agent a slip of paper as he was leaving for his home, telling him to read it at his leisure. It was a written conveyance of that tract of land, nearly eleven hundred acres; thus showing Washington's great generosity as well as his humor.

LOVE

To the distinguished character of a Patriot, it should be our highest glory to add the more distinguished character of a Christian.

*W*HEN PEOPLE THINK OF George Washington they do not usually think of love as a distinguishing character trait, because they have an emotional, romantic notion of love, not a biblical view. The apostle Paul writes in 1 Corinthians 13:4–8, "Love suffers long and is kind; love does not envy; love does not parade itself, is not puffed up; does not behave rudely, does not seek its own, is not provoked, thinks no evil; does not rejoice in iniquity, but rejoices in the truth; bears all things, believes all things, hopes all things, endures all things. Love never fails." As evidenced in the character qualities of Washington already considered, this statement depicts the man's life precisely. The more one learns about Washington, the more one sees an example of Paul's description of perfect love.

Love is not puffed up. A man who accomplishes little may easily demonstrate this quality. Washington had more reason to be puffed up than any other person because he accomplished such great things and was so popular, yet he remained humble. He did not seek his own—he did not fight against those seeking to displace him with a new commander during the war, nor did he seek to preserve his position. He did nothing and was vindicated. When Thomas Conway and others formed an alliance against him, he did not take into account a wrong suffered. At times when he was reviled, he only blessed in return. Washington suffered greatly and endured without complaint.

Love is a conscious decision to live life in service to others, as opposed to seeking that others would make one's own life easier. Washington did not seek his own comfort and security; instead, he served his country and others. He did not fail in the tasks he undertook; he succeeded because of his understanding of biblical love.

The Bible teaches that if we love God, we will keep His commandments. Washington demonstrated his love by respecting and living in accordance with the commands of God, in particular the Ten Commandments. Every Sunday, when attending Pohick or Christ's Church, Washington saw the Ten Commandments prominently displayed on the wall of the sanctuary. He had been taught these from his youth and believed that all men should obey these fundamental laws of the Creator if they hoped to be happy. Obedience to God's law brings life, to people and nations. Washington's life, words, and orders reflect this view.

From the first general orders to the troops issued by Washington on July 4, 1775, the soldiers immediately learned of his character and his expectation that they should act like Christians. After stating the need for discipline and subordination among the army, he said: "The General most earnestly requires, and expects, a due observance of those articles of war, established for the Government of the army, which forbid profane cursing, swearing, and drunkenness; And in like manner he requires and expects, of all Officers, and Soldiers, not engaged on actual duty, a punctual attendance on divine Service, to implore the blessing of heaven upon the means used for our safety and defence."[336]

In essence, he was encouraging them to observe the first four commandments. At various other times, he encouraged his soldiers to live in accordance with the principles contained in all the commandments. He recognized that what made a good soldier was the same that made a good Christian: someone who obeyed God's commandments. On July 9, 1776, the general orders included, "The General hopes and trusts that every officer and man will endeavor so to live and act as becomes a Christian soldier."[337] At Valley Forge, he reminded his soldiers: "To the distinguished character of a Patriot, it should be our highest glory to add the more distinguished character of a Christian."[338]

A Christian soldier was one who feared and worshiped God, remembered the Sabbath, honored his parents, did not steal or murder, promoted a biblical understanding of family life, and sought the well-being of his neighbor; that is, he kept the commandments. Washington powerfully demonstrated these qualities in his own words and deeds: he loved God and his neighbor.

PART 3

THE LEGACY OF GEORGE WASHINGTON

I have only been an instrument in the hands of Providence, to effect . . . a revolution which is interesting to the general liberties of mankind, and to the emancipation of a country which may afford an Asylum . . . to the oppressed and needy of the Earth.

GEORGE WASHINGTON

His example is complete; and it will teach wisdom and virtue to Magistrates, Citizens, and Men, not only in the present age, but in future generations.

—JOHN ADAMS

"An Instrument in the Hands of Providence"

*G*EORGE WASHINGTON WAS ONE of the greatest men in history. Thomas Jefferson said: "On the whole, his character was, in its mass perfect, in nothing bad, in a few points indifferent; and it may be truly said that never did nature and fortune combine more perfectly to make a man great, and to place him in the same constellation with whatever worthies have merited from man an everlasting remembrance."[1]

Regarding Washington's legacy, Jefferson went on to say:

> For his was the singular destiny and merit of leading the armies of his country successfully through an arduous war, for the establishment of its independence; of conducting its councils through the birth of a government new in its forms and principles, until it had settled down into a quiet and orderly train; and of scrupulously obeying the laws through the whole of his career, civil and military, of

which the history of the world furnishes no other example. . . . I felt, on his death, with my countrymen, that
"verily a great man hath fallen this day in Israel."²

After Washington's death, hundreds of orations were
given all over the country before local and state authorities,
at universities, and at many churches. Many of these were
published. Nearly all of them declared that Washington
was a gift from God to the American people and to all
mankind. Some mention this in passing, but for many this
was the dominant theme. Washington was called the
Moses of the American people, the Joshua who led his
people into the promised land, and the savior of his coun-
try.³ The Reverend Phillips Payson said in his sermon to the
town of Chelsea on the day they paid tribute to Washington: "The period having arrived in the course of providence, when we should be freed from a foreign yoke, and
our great revolution commence; . . . that God who formed
Moses to be the deliverer of his people, from their bondage
in Egypt, that God who taught the hands of David to war,
. . . that God, formed, endowed and assisted George Washington, a native of Virginia, to be the deliverer of his country, and perform wonders, which astonish the world."⁴

In his sermon "On the Death of George Washington,"
the Reverend Jedidiah Morse concluded his comparison of
Moses and Washington by saying: "Never, perhaps, were
coincidences in character and fortune, between any two illustrious men who have lived, so numerous and so striking,
as between Moses and Washington. . . . Both were born for
great and similar achievements; to deliver, under the guidance of Providence, each the tribes of their respective

countrymen, from the yoke of oppression, and to establish them, with the best form of government and the wisest code of laws, an independent and respectable nation."[5]

Those delivering these orations recognized God's hand in Washington's life and in directing the affairs of history and advancing liberty, which is in great contrast to many historians of the twentieth century and since.

Gen. Daniel Morgan, who fought alongside Washington during the Revolutionary War, acknowledged that Washington was the key for America's obtaining independence. He related to G. W. P. Custis that while there were many officers with great talents, Washington was "necessary, to guide, direct, and animate the whole, and it pleased Almighty God to send that one in the person of George Washington!"[6]

Leaders in other nations recognized Washington's greatness. Parliamentarian Charles James Fox, addressing the British Parliament in 1794, spoke of the illustrious Washington, "before whom all borrowed greatness sinks into insignificance, and all the potentates of Europe . . . become little and contemptible!"[7] English Lord Thomas Erskine wrote to Washington in 1795: "You are the only human being for whom I ever felt an awful reverence. I sincerely pray God to grant a long and serene evening to a life so gloriously devoted to the universal happiness of the world."[8] Napoleon Bonaparte commented: "Washington's measure of fame is full. Posterity will talk of him with reverence as the founder of a great empire, when my name shall be lost in the vortex of Revolutions."[9]

President Calvin Coolidge summed up Washington's contribution to mankind, under the providence of God, in a February 22, 1927, speech to Congress: "Washington was the directing spirit without which there would have been no independence, no Union, no Constitution and no Republic. His ways were the ways of truth. His influence grows. In wisdom of action, in purity of character he stands alone. We cannot yet estimate him. We can only indicate our reverence for him and thank the Divine Providence which sent him to serve and inspire his fellow men."[10]

Washington's contribution to the birth of America and the advancement of liberty in the world is unsurpassed by any other man. Without Washington, America would not have won the Revolution. He provided the leadership necessary to hold the troops together, even in the most difficult situations, as at Valley Forge. As one contemporary observed, Washington was "that hero, who affected, with little bloodshed, the greatest revolution in history."[11] Due to Washington's influence, America avoided a monarchy or military rule—he rebuffed an attempt to make him king, he thwarted a military coup, and he set an example of civilian rule by resigning as commander in chief. The Constitutional Convention would not have succeeded without Washington's influence as president of that body. America may never have set in motion its constitutional form of government, with a limited role of the president, without his example, for the unanimously elected Washington modeled how presidents were to govern. Washington also set the standard for American international relations in his Farewell Address.

There would be no America, the land of liberty, without Washington, the apostle of liberty. The unique freedom, justice, and virtue incorporated into the American Republic have in the last two centuries spread across the world and taken root in many nations. Hence, Washington's legacy has impacted the world and will continue to do so for centuries to come.

His greatness did not stem from oratorical skills or superior knowledge or brilliant military tactics, but rather from his strong virtues, sense of duty, and invincible resolution. When he was offered leadership of the army and leadership of the nation, he expressed doubts in his abilities to accomplish these tasks, but once he occupied those positions, nothing could stop him from performing his duty. By sheer force of character he held the disorganized nation together during the great struggle for independence, and after victory was won, the love of the people for him provided the unifying factor necessary to set a course for the American constitutional republic.

The providence of God and Washington's Christian faith were key to his character, career, and accomplishments. His faith, heart, and humility are revealed in the "Circular to the Governors of the States" in 1783 when he prayed that God would protect them and "most graciously be pleased to dispose us all to do justice, to love mercy, and to demean ourselves with that charity, humility, and pacific temper of mind, which were the characteristics of the Divine Author of our blessed religion, and without an humble imitation of whose example in these things, we can never hope to be a happy nation."[12]

In his famous "Oration on the Death of General Washington," Gen. Henry Lee said that Washington was "first in war, first in peace, and first in the hearts of his countrymen."

"Vice shuddered in his presence, and virtue always felt his fostering hand; the purity of his private character gave effulgence to his public virtues." Washington was first because, as Lee said, he was "the man designed by Heaven to lead in the great political, as well as military, events which have distinguished the area of his life. The finger of an overruling Providence pointing at Washington was neither mistaken nor unobserved."[13]

Washington himself had a sense of how God used him providentially to advance the cause of liberty to mankind as well as an understanding of the providential purpose of America, writing in March 1785: "At best I have only been an instrument in the hands of Providence, to effect, with the aid of France and many virtuous fellow Citizens of America, a revolution which is interesting to the general liberties of mankind, and to the emancipation of a country which may afford an Asylum, if we are wise enough to pursue the paths wch. lead to virtue and happiness, to the oppressed and needy of the Earth."[14]

America set in motion a new example of religious, civil, and economic liberty that the nations of the world have attempted to embrace over the last two centuries. The advancement of liberty in the world is directly related to the establishment of liberty in America, which owes its beginnings in large part to George Washington. Thomas Paine's epithet of "World's Apostle of Liberty" is, therefore, most fitting. Americans and all citizens of the world who value liberty must forever keep alive in their hearts this great man and seek to follow his example.

A HUMAN EXAMPLE TO IMITATE

*His example: that let us endeavor, by delineating,
to impart to mankind. Virtue will place it in her
temple, Wisdom in her treasury.*

—FISHER AMES

EARLIER WE NOTED THAT George Washington
was so revered that John Adams feared some
people were making a god out of him. Yet as the boy who
met Washington on the street in Philadelphia remarked,
he was just a man, and of course, he was just that. But
with the hand of Providence and his Christian character,
Washington participated in and directed events of such
significance that he was elevated to a position among the
foremost men in history.

Washington was not a stoic icon to be placed upon a
pedestal and worshiped. He was a man who enjoyed life
and its pleasures, but he put others and duty to country
above himself. He feared God and was a faithful Christian, though he was not a sectarian. He did not leave a
precise set of doctrines that he believed others should follow, but he lived a life of faith, demonstrating to others
the fruit of Christianity.

People often remarked that Washington emanated a presence. Chaplain of the Congress Ashbel Green wrote, "There was more of the indefinable quality called presence in President Washington, than any other person I have ever known."[15] This presence was largely caused by his strong faith and character.

He had faults that he had to overcome. He had strong passions that he had to govern. He made decisions that did not always prove to be the best. He had enemies (or those who resisted him), but these were largely those who disagreed with his military tactics or held opposing political beliefs, rather than opposing him for lack of character.

He was confident, as was necessary to accomplish such great things, but he was not arrogant. Washington was a man of great virtue, but he was also one who had no vices that overshadowed his virtues. As all confident men of strength and ambition, he showed signs of youthful pride, but he quickly grew out of this. He displayed biblical qualities of love.

Washington's great influence was not due to any one talent, skill, or accomplishment, but "it is the happy combination of rare talents and qualities, the harmonious union of the intellectual and moral powers, rather than the dazzling splendor of any one trait, which constitute the grandeur of his character."[16]

Though he was a man, he was one who should be imitated in that he reflected many biblical qualities of character. He was not perfect, but he was an example of one who learned to govern himself and subject his life to the principles of godliness. He highly valued life, liberty, and property.

Though too humble to ever express it, he could have said, "Imitate me!" Americans formerly learned of the Father of their Country and many imitated him. (Even if some early biographies idealized him, it brought great benefit to all who mimicked this high standard.) Today, few Americans know the man and thus are deprived of an example of principle and character whose ideas and qualities are desperately needed by the nation. He was to the world the epitome of America. For America to survive as the most free, prosperous, just, and virtuous nation in history, she needs to know her father and imitate him. Washington should ever live in the hearts of the American people.

THE LESSONS OF LEADERSHIP

∂ Christianity is the source of liberty, happiness, and prosperity in society. Leaders have a duty to acknowledge God and obey His will.

∂ Without moral leadership, free nations cannot endure. Without morality in the people, there will be no morality in the leaders.

∂ Godly, moral leaders do not arise by chance; they are raised up by the providence of God to fulfill their destiny, which contributes to God's overall plan for mankind.

∂ The strength of a leader resides in his ability to be self-governed. One must learn to govern himself before he can effectively govern others.

∂ Godly leaders will never seek to usurp power but only to use that which is delegated to them and is necessary to accomplish the ends for which it was given.

∂ Obedience is the habit of submitting one's will and actions to that which is right. The homes of a nation are the seminaries of obedient citizens and leaders.

❧ Godly obedience entails not just outward action but internal submission of the heart.

❧ Good civil leaders should not only have excellent character; they should also have a knowledge of the truth, especially in regard to public affairs and governmental philosophy.

❧ Man, under God, is the source of power within a society, not the government or civil leaders.

❧ Civil leaders recognize that their purpose is to protect the God-given rights of every citizen to life, liberty, and property. The rights of conscience, especially in regard to worship, are of primary importance.

❧ Principled education is necessary for a leader to make a positive contribution to society.

❧ To secure peace, a nation must always be ready for war.

❧ Elected representatives should govern from principle, not political pressure.

❧ Leaders are courageous, "incapable of fear, meeting personal dangers with the calmest unconcern."

❧ A sense of duty—to God and to country—and a heart to serve are the motivation of a godly leader. Leaders will seek to serve others rather than rule over them.

❧ Leaders place the good of their fellow citizens and nation above their own pleasure.

❧ Leaders are willing to sacrifice much for the higher obligations to God and country.

∞ Anyone who fails to fulfill his duties and responsibilities in the home, while seeking to lead in other areas of activity, fails overall as a leader.

∞ The character of a leader gives value and force to his words.

∞ Habitual diligence, or steady attention to the business at hand, is an essential characteristic of a good leader.

∞ He who is diligent in the little things will be able to lead in large affairs.

∞ Leaders never quit but maintain a never-yielding perseverance and determination regardless of how difficult the circumstances.

∞ When the situation requires it, a leader is kind and tender. He is always full of compassion.

∞ A leader is confident in his abilities, but always humble, recognizing his shortcomings and need for help.

∞ Greatness is revealed in a leader's humble response to high praise.

∞ The people of a free nation must be honest, having a disposition to conform to correct moral principles or truth.

∞ A leader gives his time, money, and talent with no thought of return.

∞ A wise leader must discern that which is best, most just, and most proper. He must exercise sound judgment in attempting to do good and avoiding evil.

✍ While performing their duties in a serious way, leaders should enjoy life, people, and their calling.

✍ Good leaders make a conscious decision to live life in service to others rather than seeking their own comfort.

✍ An effective, godly leader seeks to obey God's law, and in so doing brings life to men and nations.

Notes

Full bibliographical data can be found in the bibliography.

Introduction

1. Osborn, *Washington Speaks for Himself,* xi.
2. Ames, *Works of Fisher Ames,* 527. See also, George Washington Bicentennial Commission, *History of the Bicentennial Celebration, Foreign Participation,* 211.
3. Wilbur, *Making of Washington,* 21.
4. Manship, "George Washington," 1.
5. Quoted in Osborn, *Washington Speaks for Himself,* iv.
6. Custis, *Recollections and Private Memoirs,* 511.
7. Sol Bloom in George Washington Bicentennial Commission, *History of the Bicentennial Celebration, Foreign Participation,* vii.
8. Ibid., 467.
9. Washington, *Writings,* 12:343. Hereafter cited as GWP.
10. Thomas Jefferson to Walter Jones, January 2, 1814, in Custis, *Recollections and Private Memoirs,* 214–15. Also see Sparks, *Life of Washington,* 481.
11. Irving, *Life of Washington,* 7:65–66.
12. Custis, *Recollections and Private Memoirs,* 167.

Part 1: The Life of George Washington

1. Kirkland, *Memoirs of Washington,* 13–14.
2. The family Bible records: "George Washington Son to Augustine & Mary his Wife was born the 11th Day of February 1731/2

about 10 in the Morning." The old-style date was replaced with the new-style February 22, 1732, after the British corrected the calendar in 1752, though Washington's birthday was celebrated on both days during his lifetime.

3. Kirkland, *Memoirs of Washington*, 14.

4. April 16 NS; see Freeman, *Washington*, 1:47, frontispiece.

5. See ibid., 1:64.

6. Paulding, *Life of Washington*, 1:24–34; also Kirkland, *Memoirs of Washington*, 43.

7. Paulding, *Life of Washington*, 24–34; Kirkland, *Memoirs of Washington*, 44.

8. Paulding, *Life of Washington*, 24–34; Kirkland, *Memoirs of Washington*, 45.

9. See M'Guire, *Religious Opinions and Character of Washington*, 47ff., for more on Hale's influence on Washington's character.

10. Kirkland, *Memoirs of Washington*, 53. See Weems, *History of Washington*, 37.

11. Kirkland, *Memoirs of Washington*, 55.

12. See Wilbur, *Making of Washington*, 111–18; Sparks, *Life of Washington*, 6–7; Kirkland, *Memoirs of Washington*, 66ff.; Hall, *Washington*, 145–48; and various reprints of Rules of Civility & Decent Behaviour in Company and Conversation.

13. Sparks, *Life of Washington*, 7.

14. Kirkland, *Memoirs of Washington*, 72–73.

15. Ibid., 58.

16. George Washington Bicentennial Commission, *History of the Bicentennial Celebration, Literature Series*, 31; McCullough, *1776*, 48.

17. Kirkland, *Memoirs of Washington*, 60.

18. Quoting Washington's adopted son, G. W. P. Custis, in Custis, *Recollections and Private Memoirs*, 122, 129.

19. Ibid., 131.

20. Kirkland, *Memoirs of Washington*, 47.

21. Ibid.
22. Kirkland, *Memoirs of Washington*, 80.
23. Washington, *Diaries*, 1:5.
24. Ibid., 6ff.
25. Ibid., 13.
26. Ibid., 17–18.
27. Kirkland, *Memoirs of Washington*, 86.
28. Weems, *History of Washington*, 45.
29. Washington, *Diaries*, 30–117.
30. Everett, *Washington*, 51. Jackson and Twohig wrote that Washington may have been "fortunate" that he contracted smallpox in Barbados rather than in America, because the practice of inoculation that occurred on the island had "lowered the death rate to a very small percentage" (Washington, *Diaries*, 33). Inoculation did not occur much in Virginia, but George could possibly have been inoculated in preparation for the voyage, thus making his bout with smallpox a relatively mild one (relatively mild, for many died, and many who lived carried more scars with them). Coupled with all the other divine interpositions in his life, this could better be called a "providential" rather than "fortunate" event, as Everett so declared.
31. Kirkland, *Memoirs of Washington*, 103.
32. Lawrence Washington to William Fairfax, in Washington, *Diaries*, 33.
33. See Washington, *Diaries*, 1:118, note 1.
34. Ibid., 1:147.
35. Ibid., 143–44.
36. Ibid.
37. Ibid., 155.
38. From Christopher Gist's journal, in ibid., 157.
39. Ibid., 155–56. Jared Sparks writes, "This providential escape from most imminent danger, was not the end of their calamities" (Sparks, *Life of Washington*, 31).

40. Washington, *Diaries*, 158.
41. Ibid., 163.
42. See GWP, 1:31–32.
43. Ibid., 1:35.
44. Ibid., 1:64.
45. Ibid., 1:36ff.; Washington, *Diaries*, 1:162ff.; see also Kent, *Contrecoeur's Copy of Washington's Journal*, which first appeared in *Pennsylvania History* 19, no. 1 (January 1952). Washington's journal was printed by the French after they confiscated his original; it no longer exists. The journal was translated and printed in Paris in 1756 in a form to support the French argument for seizing the Ohio region. This French edition was translated into English and published in London and in New York in 1757. Washington noted that the text was greatly distorted. This version must be compared with Washington's account submitted to Governor Dinwiddie in three letters (May 29, GWP, 1:59ff.; May 29, GWP, 1:68ff.; June 3, GWP, 1:71ff.) and a Washington letter remarking on the French edition of his journal (GWP, 1:36–37). Washington noted that a party of thirty-six men was too large for a diplomatic mission. In addition, he added that an ambassador does not need spies, two of whom were spotted and followed, enabling Washington to find their hidden encampment. The French party had remained two days within five miles of Fort Necessity without notifying him of their alleged purpose. Washington said of the later French claim that they called to the American party not to fire when they came in sight, "That I know to be False, for I was the first Man that approached them, and the first whom they saw, and immediately upon it ran to their Arms, and fir'd briskly till they were defeated" (Washington to Dinwiddie, May 29, 1754, GWP, 1:69). Not long after this, three French deserters said that a detachment was sent out to fight the English at the same time Jumonville was dispatched, reinforcing the view that he was not on a diplomatic mission (GWP, 1:73).

46. GWP, 1:70.
47. Ibid.
48. Sparks, *Life of Washington*, 46; Kirkland, *Memoirs of Washington*, 56.
49. Washington wrote: "That we were wilfully, or ignorantly, deceived by our interpreter in regard to the word assassination, I do aver, and will to my dying moment; so will every officer that was present" (GWP, 1:37).
50. Washington to William Fairfax (president of the governor's council), GWP, 1:94.
51. GWP, 1:146.
52. Ibid., 1:151.
53. Sparks, *Life of Washington*, 64.
54. Ibid., 63.
55. George Washington Parke Custis noted that even more bullets pierced Washington's clothing: "The hat worn on that eventful day, and which was pierced by two balls, was at Mount Vernon, and both seen and handled by several persons, long within our remembrance" (Custis, *Recollections and Private Memoirs*, 304).
56. Headley, *Illustrated Life of Washington*, 59.
57. Custis, *Recollections and Private Memoirs*, 304, see also 223–24.
58. GWP, 1:152. In preparation for the potential publication of his papers, Washington rewrote his correspondence in 1784/85 in which he used this wording: "But by the all powerful dispensatns. of Providence, I have been protected beyond all human probability and expectation; for I had 4 Bullets through my Coat, and two Horses shot under me, and yet escaped unhurt, although death was levelling my companions on every side of me" (see GWP, 1:152, note 44, and Irving, *Life of Washington*, 1:259).
59. GWP, 1:153; see also Davies, *Religion and Patriotism*; Custis, *Recollections and Private Memoirs*, 304.

60. This story was formerly used in school texts as an example of the providence of God. While in some Christian textbooks today, it can no longer be found in the textbooks of today's public schools.
61. GWP, 1:152.
62. Sparks, *Life of Washington*, 65.
63. Washington to Robert Jackson, August 2, 1755, GWP, 1:155.
64. Braddock's defeat also encouraged the organization of volunteer companies throughout Virginia. Ministers encouraged this martial spirit. Samuel Davies's sermon, mentioned earlier in the text, to one of these companies referred to Washington and his providential preservation.
65. Americans today cannot appreciate how advancements in medicine have alleviated many afflictions that colonials faced regularly. Throughout his life, Washington suffered numerous illnesses, many for extended periods.
66. Kirkland, *Memoirs of Washington*, 166.
67. Ibid., 144; see GWP, 1:117.
68. McDowell, *In God We Trust*, 73.
69. GWP, 12:343.
70. Irving, *Life of Washington*, 1:191.
71. Some writers have suggested that Washington was in love with Sally Cary Fairfax, the wife of his friend George William Fairfax, and may have entertained inappropriate relations with her. When he was seventeen, George wrote of being smitten by a "Lowland beauty" to whom he never revealed his feelings. Some have believed this was Sally Cary. Some have said he expressed his love to her in a September 12, 1758, letter (see GWP, 2:287–89; and Henriques, *America's First President*, 16), but this is not clear. While Washington liked Sally, they certainly had no inappropriate relations, and he put aside any youthful attachment in a manly way. Washington and Martha Washington remained close friends with the Fairfaxes. Washington had enjoyed the company of ladies but not in an inappropriate way. On

a trip to Boston during the French and Indian War, Washington was charmed by Mary Phillips of New York. Some believe he considered matrimony, but she married another (Sparks, *Life of Washington*, 73).

72. Custis, *Recollections and Private Memoirs*, 509.
73. Kirkland, *Memoirs of Washington*, 191.
74. For more on this, see McDowell, *Building Godly Nations*, 96–98.
75. See Adams, *Rights of the Colonists*.
76. Washington to Bryan Fairfax, July 20, 1774, GWP, 3:232–33.
77. Kirkland, *Memoirs of Washington*, 216.
78. Ibid., 215.
79. Washington, *Diaries*, 2:254.
80. For more on this prayer and other events leading up to the war, see McDowell, *Building Godly Nations*, 96–103; Beliles and Mc-Dowell, *America's Providential History*, 127–46.
81. Custis, *Recollections and Private Memoirs*, 156; Kirkland, *Memoirs of Washington*, 220.
82. "Proceedings of the Virginia Convention," 12–13. See also Kirkland, *Memoirs of Washington*, 221.
83. Washington to George William Fairfax, May 31, 1775, GWP, 3:291–92.
84. John Adams to Abigail Adams, June 17, 1775, in Adams, *Book of Abigail and John*, 89.
85. GWP, 3:292.
86. Ibid.
87. Ibid., 292–93.
88. Ibid., 3:294.
89. Kirkland, *Memoirs of Washington*, 233.
90. Ibid., 234.
91. GWP, 3:309.
92. Washington to the president of Congress, September 21, 1775, GWP, 3:512.
93. Kirkland, *Memoirs of Washington*, 250.

94. GWP, 4:243.
95. Kirkland, *Memoirs of Washington*, 269.
96. Ibid.
97. Washington to Josiah Quincy, March 24, 1776, GWP 4:421.
98. GWP, 4:441–42.
99. Johnston, *Washington Day by Day*, 41, quoted in Johnson, *Washington*, 78.
100. See Love, *Fast and Thanksgiving Days of New England*; and McDowell, *America, a Christian Nation?* 27–28, 48–49.
101. GWP, 5:245.
102. Ibid., 5:244–45.
103. Washington to the president of Congress, August 31, 1776, ibid., 5:506.
104. Irving, *Life of Washington*, 2:306.
105. Ibid., 2:317, 310–17.
106. Washington to the president of Congress, September 2, 1776, GWP, 6:4.
107. Irving, *Life of Washington*, 2:332.
108. Washington to Lund Washington, December 10, 1776, GWP, 6:347.
109. Sparks, *Life of Washington*, 205.
110. Ibid., 206.
111. GWP, 6:398–99.
112. Sparks (*Life of Washington*, 212) reports that two were killed in the fighting and two froze to death.
113. Custis, *Recollections and Private Memoirs*, 190.
114. Ibid., 251.
115. Ibid., 190; Sparks, *Life of Washington*, 218.
116. Sparks, *Life of Washington*, 241; see also Custis, *Recollections and Private Memoirs*, 208.
117. Washington to John A. Washington, October 18, 1777, GWP, 9:399; Johnson, *Washington*, 100.
118. See Custis, *Recollections and Private Memoirs*, 210.

119. GWP, 10:167.
120. Morris, *Christian Life and Character of the Civil Institutions of the United States*, 530–31.
121. GWP, 10:168.
122. Washington to Lafayette, December 31, 1777, GWP, 10:237.
123. See Custis, *Recollections and Private Memoirs*, 275; Weems, *History of Washington*, 300–301; the testimony of The Reverend Devault Beaver in M'Guire, *Religious Opinions and Character of Washington*, 158; and the testimony of Dr. N. R. Snowden in Wylie, *Washington a Christian*, 28–29.
124. Johnson, *Washington*, 106.
125. Ibid., 106–7.
126. Kirkland, *Memoirs of Washington*, 343.
127. Ibid., 349.
128. GWP, 12:343.
129. Sparks, *Life of Washington*, 286.
130. Ibid., 283, 295–96.
131. Washington to Joseph Reed, June 25, 1780, GWP, 19:70.
132. Kirkland, *Memoirs of Washington*, 372.
133. Washington to the president of Congress, October 13, 1780, GWP, 20:173.
134. Washington to William Heath, September 26, 1780, GWP, 20:88–89.
135. Washington to the president of Congress, September 26, 1780, GWP, 20:92.
136. Washington to John Laurens, October 13, 1780, GWP, 20:173.
137. GWP, 20:95.
138. Journals of Congress, October 18, 1780, in Beliles and McDowell, *America's Providential History*, 165.
139. Washington to John Laurens, October 13, 1780, GWP, 20:173.
140. Parts of the following chapter are adapted from the author's book *America's Providential History* and are used by permission.
141. McDowell, *America's Providential History*, 167.

142. Ibid.

143. General orders, October 20, 1781, GWP 23:245, 247.

144. General orders, April 18, 1783, GWP, 26:334.

145. Farewell Orders to the Armies of the United States, November 2, 1783, GWP, 27:223–26.

146. "Circular to the Governors of the States," June 8, 1783, GWP, 26:496.

147. Sparks, *Life of Washington*, 371.

148. Kirkland, *Memoirs of Washington*, 116.

149. Washington to John Rodgers, June 11, 1783, GWP, 27:1.

150. Washington to Henry Knox, February 20, 1784, GWP, 27:340–41.

151. Washington to Marquis De Lafayette, February 1, 1784, GWP, 27:318.

152. Sparks, *Life of Washington*, 523.

153. Kirkland, *Memoirs of Washington*, 416; Custis, *Recollections and Private Memoirs*, 421.

154. Custis, *Recollections and Private Memoirs*, 171, 508.

155. Washington to Henry Knox, January 5, 1785, GWP 28:23.

156. Custis, *Recollections and Private Memoirs*, 373.

157. Washington to Alexander Hamilton, March 31, 1783, GWP, 26:277.

158. See Washington to James Warren, October 7, 1785, GWP, 28:289–92.

159. GWP, 28:503.

160. Ibid.

161. Sparks, *Life of Washington*, 394.

162. Washington to Henry Knox, April 27, 1787, GWP, 29:208–9.

163. Washington to James Madison, March 31, 1787, GWP, 29:191–92; Sparks, *Life of Washington*, 401–2.

164. Fiske, *Critical Period*, 275.

165. Madison, *Notes*, 209–10.

166. Farrand, *Records*, 3:471. Alexander Hamilton opposed the reso-

lution, saying such an action at that time might communicate to the public (who knew nothing of the events in the closed convention) that the delegates were having troubles, and such news might undermine the popular support for the convention. Roger Sherman of Connecticut pointed out that the delegates would have greater troubles if they neglected this important duty. It was also proposed to have a sermon preached on July 4 at the request of the convention. Jonathan Dayton recorded that the chaplain motion was seconded and carried; James Madison recorded that the delegates did not vote on the issue. If this were so, it was because they had no funds to officially invite a chaplain, as pointed out by Hugh Williamson of North Carolina (see Madison, *Notes*, 210–11.) Note that chaplains were obtained in some manner, since they began opening the daily sessions with prayer (see Farrand, *Records*, 472).

167. Farrand, *Records*, 472.
168. The *North American Review* in 1867 stated: "The American government and Constitution is the most precious possession which the world holds, or which the future can inherit. This is true—true because the American system is the political expression of Christian ideas." For more on the convention and the Constitution, see Beliles and Anderson, *Contending for the Constitution.*
169. Sparks, *Life of Washington*, 403; see also Washington to Henry Knox, August 19, 1787, GWP, 29:261, and Washington to Patrick Henry, September 24, 1787, GWP, 29:278.
170. Sparks, *Life of Washington*, 403.
171. Washington to Thomas Jefferson, August 23, 1792, GWP, 32:131.
172. Washington to Jonathan Trumbull, July 20, 1788, GWP, 30:22.
173. Jared Sparks observed: "George Washington was chosen, by the unanimous vote of the electors, and probably without a dissenting voice in the whole nation" (*Life of Washington*, 406).

174. Sparks, *Life of Washington*, 407.

175. GWP, 30:285.

176. Ibid., 30:287.

177. Ames, *Works of Fisher Ames*, 567.

178. See Lossing, *Mount Vernon and Its Associations*, 202.

179. Morris, *Christian Life and Character of the Civil Institutions of the United States*, 271.

180. Custis, *Recollections and Private Memoirs*, 395.

181. Sparks, *Life of Washington*, 410, 415.

182. Ibid., 419.

183. Thomas Jefferson to Washington, May 23, 1792, in Jefferson, *Writings*, 8:347–48.

184. Sparks, *Life of Washington*, 444.

185. Ibid.

186. See McDowell, *Building Godly Nations*, chaps. 4, 6, 7, 11.

187. Another event that brought attacks on Washington was his signing a treaty with Great Britain in 1795 that expressed his neutrality in the rising conflict between France and Britain. Many opposed this treaty, and party discord increased greatly, with some even attacking Washington's motives and character. Yet it kept the country out of war, a war America could not afford to fight, and allowed the U.S. economy to increase. In hindsight, it was another sound decision by the president.

188. Eighth Annual Address, December 7, 1796, in Richardson, *Messages and Papers of the Presidents*, 1:196.

189. GWP, 35:455–56.

190. Washington to G. W. P. Custis, July 10, 1797, ibid., 35:494.

191. Sparks, *Life of Washington*, 483.

192. GWP, 36:313.

193. Tobias Lear, "Last Illness and Death of Washington," in Sparks, *Life of Washington*, 531–35.

194. Custis, *Recollections and Private Memoirs*, 398; Irving, *Life of Washington*, 5:21.

195. See Custis, *Recollections and Private Memoirs*, 510.
196. Lear, "Last Illness and Death of Washington," in Sparks, *Life of Washington*, 531–35.
197. Sparks, *Life of Washington*, 536–38.
198. Custis, *Recollections and Private Memoirs*, 439, 384. George and Martha Washington and other members of their family are buried there.
199. The Mount Vernon Ladies' Association collected about seven hundred of these eulogies in the Jackson Collection; see Holmes, *A Nation Mourns*, 10. Various books of compilations of orations and sermons have been published; see, for example: *Memory of Washington*; *Eulogies and Orations*; and *Selection of Orations and Eulogies*.
200. See for example, Willard, *Address in Latin*.
201. Sparks, *Life of Washington*, 539.
202. Ibid., 541.

PART 2: THE CHARACTER OF GEORGE WASHINGTON

1. Meade, *Old Churches, Ministers and Families of Virginia*, 2:243.
2. Schroeder, *Maxims of George Washington* (1989), 164.
3. Schroeder, *Maxims of George Washington* (1854), 340.
4. See, e.g., Flexner, *Forge of Experience*, 243–45, who references Boller, *Washington and Religion*. Many other writers also have looked to Boller's work when presenting Washington's faith. Other writers, such as Ellis, *His Excellency*, give brief mention of his faith, saying he was at best a nominal Episcopalian. To support his view, Ellis points out that Washington used phrases such as "divine providence" instead of God, he did not take communion, and he stood to pray. And yet we know that Washington did use words such as God, Christ, and eighty other terms for God; he did take communion (although he did not take communion while he was president, but not because he denied the faith); and many saw him pray on his knees, while sitting, and while standing at meals, etc.

5. A few who affirmed his Christian faith include John Marshall, Aaron Bancroft, Mason Weems, Washington Irving, Jared Sparks, David Ramsay, James Paulding, George Washington Parke Custis, Benson Lossing, and John C. Fitzpatrick.

6. See, e.g., Holmes, *A Nation Mourns.*

7. For example, E. C. M'Guire wrote: "The peculiar and excellent virtues distinguishing this favoured servant of God, could not be ascribed to any other source, than the grace of the Holy Spirit" (*Religious Opinions and Character of Washington*, 404).

8. See Johnson, *Washington;* M'Guire, *Religious Opinions and Character of Washington;* Littell, *Washington—Christian;* Wylie, *Washington a Christian;* Novak and Novak, *Washington's God;* Slaughter, *Christianity the Key to the Character and Career of Washington.*

9. John Marshall, *The Life of George Washington*, 2:445, quoted in Hall, *Washington*, 11.

10. Schroeder, *Maxims of George Washington* (1855), 367.

11. *Eulogies and Orations*, 37, from a eulogy by Jonathan Mitchell Sewall, December 31, 1799, in Barton, *Freemasonry and the Founding Fathers*, 111; see also in M'Guire, *Religious Opinions and Character of Washington*, 358.

12. Gunning Bedford, quoted in Barton, *Freemasonry and the Founding Fathers*, 101.

13. Washington, *Writings*, 12:406–7; see also Sparks, *Life of Washington*, 522.

14. Muhlenberg, *Journals*, 3:149.

15. Jarratt quoted in M'Guire, *Religious Opinions and Character of Washington*, 393; Meade, *Old Churches, Ministers and Families of Virginia*, 245; Schroeder, *Maxims of George Washington* (1855), 367; Johnson, *Washington*, 256.

16. Sparks, *Life of Washington*, 523.

17. M'Guire, *Religious Opinions and Character of Washington*, 141–42.

18. Sparks, *Life of Washington*, 492.
19. Bancroft quoted in Hall, *Washington*, 12.
20. Johnson, *Washington*, 166–67.
21. Custis, *Recollections and Private Memoirs*, 173.
22. Some modern writers have reported that Washington missed church many times, concluding that this shows a lack of true Christian belief. They overlook the testimony of family and friends, and fail to take into account the obstacles posed by weather in making the trip to church each week.
23. Sparks, *Life of Washington*, 521.
24. GWP, 37:484–85.
25. Washington, *Diaries*, 3:280, 284, 285, 286.
26. Johnson, *Washington*, 89.
27. Sparks, *Life of Washington*, 521.
28. Custis, *Recollections and Private Memoirs*, 508.
29. Ibid., 171.
30. Sparks, *Life of Washington*, 519–20.
31. Meade, *Old Churches, Ministers and Families of Virginia*, 245.
32. Washington to Benedict Arnold, September 14, 1775, GWP, 3:492.
33. See GWP, 27:342, 30:467 for two examples.
34. See Johnson, *Washington*, 288–91; Novak and Novak, *Washington's God*, 243–45.
35. GWP, 23:478.
36. Washington to Marquis de Chastellux, April 25, 1788, GWP, 29:485.
37. GWP, 27:317.
38. See, e.g., GWP, 35:432, 447, 452.
39. GWP, 27:128.
40. Washington to George Washington Parke Custis, November 15, 1796, in Custis, *Recollections and Private Memoirs*, 74.
41. For a list, see Hall, *Washington*, 254–71.
42. Johnson, *Washington*, 23–35.

43. Sparks, *Life of Washington*, 523; see also Morris, *Christian Life and Character of the Civil Institutions of the United States*, 501–2, for another testimony from Lewis.

44. Sparks, *Life of Washington*, 522.

45. "Circular to the Governors of the States," June 8, 1783, GWP, 26:496.

46. Johnson, *Washington*, 231.

47. Washington, *Diaries*, 3:254.

48. Custis, *Recollections and Private Memoirs*, 173.

49. Meade, *Old Churches, Ministers and Families of Virginia*, 245.

50. See Johnson, *Washington*, 61.

51. Custis, *Recollections and Private Memoirs*, 398.

52. Sparks, *Life of Washington*, 545.

53. M'Guire, *Religious Opinions and Character of Washington*, 158.

54. *London Chronicle*, September 21–23, 1779, quoted in Johnson, *Washington*, 120–21.

55. Johnson, *Washington*, 163.

56. Jones, *Ashbel Green*, 267.

57. Custis, *Recollections and Private Memoirs*, 435.

58. Washington, *Diaries*, 3:254.

59. Johnson, *Washington*, 144.

60. GWP, 3:308.

61. Ibid., 27:227.

62. Jones, *Ashbel Green*, 270.

63. Richardson, *Messages and Papers of the Presidents*, 1:56.

64. See Force, *American Archives*, 5th ser., 1:226; see also GWP, 5:244–45.

65. Kirkland, *Memoirs of Washington*, 237; Johnson, *Washington*, 69–70.

66. GWP, 4:369.

67. General orders for May 2, 1778, ibid., 11:343.

68. GWP, 5:367. He issued similar orders during the French and Indian War; see Sparks, *Life of Washington*, 519.

69. Orders for May 26, 1777, in Johnson, *Washington*, 98.

70. Orders for May 16, 1782, GWP, 24:260.

71. General Orders, March 22, 1783, ibid., 26:250.

72. Custis, *Recollections and Private Memoirs*, 376, 162.

73. M'Guire, *Religious Opinions and Character of Washington*, 138; Schroeder, *Maxims of Washington* (1855), 377.

74. Sparks, *Life of Washington*, 278.

75. See Lossing, *Mount Vernon and Its Associations*, 202.

76. Washington to the Reverend John Rodgers, June 11, 1783, GWP, 27:1.

77. GWP, 26:496; see pages 165–73, "Christian Character and Morality".

78. See GWP, 30:291ff.

79. Richardson, *Messages and Papers of the Presidents*, 1:205–16.

80. Custis, *Recollections and Private Memoirs*, 290.

81. See, e.g., GWP, 30:336, 339, 416; Washington, *Washington's Addresses to the Churches*.

82. Sparks, *Life of Washington*, 525.

83. GWP, 15:55.

84. Johnson, *Washington*, 169; GWP, 30:355.

85. Washington, *Writings*, 12:405–7; Sparks, *Life of Washington*, 522.

86. Sparks, *Life of Washington*, 520.

87. Ibid., 525.

88. GWP, 15:55.

89. See Johnson, *Washington*, 288–91; and Novak and Novak, *Washington's God*, 243–45.

90. See Holmes, *A Nation Mourns*. Note that the Reverend James Madison's religious terminology is similar to Washington's, using "Providence" and other nonevangelical words.

91. *An American Dictionary of the English Language* (1828), s.v. "Providence."

92. For example, in his first inaugural address; he later uses "providential" in reverence to this.

93. From the eulogy given by Jonathan Mitchell Sewall on December 31, 1799, in *Eulogies and Orations* (1800), 37.

94. See Johnson, *Washington*, 96–98.

95. Ibid., 244. For others, see Sparks, *Life of Washington*, 524; Meade, *Old Churches, Ministers and Families of Virginia*, 490–492; Johnson, *Washington*, 58, 85–86, 89ff., 194–95.

96. The minister of the Philadelphia church Washington attended while president may have expressed some concern that he did not take communion. One of the first ministers to question his faith was Episcopal minister Bird Wilson in 1831. He asserted that Washington was not a professor of religion, but he also claimed that no president to that point had professed religion, which was not an accurate statement. Around this same time, socialist Robert Owen also questioned Washington's faith, but Owen had an agenda to change America from a self-governed republic to a socialistic utopia.

97. Contrary to the popular image, less than 20 percent of the Founding Fathers were Masons; see Barton, *Freemasonry and the Founding Fathers*.

98. See Barton, *Freemasonry and the Founding Fathers*, 59–61; and William Adrian Brown, *When & Where: A Chronology of the Life of George Washington*, discussed in Manship, "George Washington," 1–8.

99. William Wirt quoted in Barton, *Freemasonry and the Founding Fathers*, 30.

100. Cited in ibid., 37.

101. Quoted in ibid., 39.

102. Quoted in ibid., 39.

103. Quoted in ibid., 39.

104. Quoted in ibid., 40.

105. Quoted in ibid., 41.

106. Ibid., 40–43.

107. Ibid., 45–47.

108. Quoted in ibid., 44.

109. Manship, "George Washington," 7–8.

110. See GWP, 36:453, and Washington, *Writings*, 11:314.

111. Washington, *Writings*, 11:314.

112. GWP, 36:453; Washington, *Writings*, 11:314–15. For more on the attempts of the Illuminati to come into America, see Barton, *Freemasonry and the Founding Fathers*, 53.

113. See GWP, 36:518–19.

114. Washington to Robert Morris, April 12, 1786, GWP 28:408.

115. See McDowell, *Building Godly Nations*, 219–22.

116. Ibid., 221.

117. Irving, *Life of Washington*, 1:355–56.

118. Hall, *Washington*, 107.

119. Washington to Lawrence Lewis, August 4, 1797, GWP 36:2.

120. Letter on November 23, 1794, ibid., 34:47.

121. Letter on September 9, 1786, ibid., 29:5.

122. Letter on August 18, 1799, ibid., 37:338.

123. See Fitzpatrick, *Last Will and Testament of Washington*, 2–4; and Sparks, *Life of Washington*, 545–62. In his will, Washington freed his slaves "upon the decease of my wife." Any action prior to his death would have caused problems, because many of his slaves had mixed with those who had been owned by Martha prior to her marriage to Washington, and he had no authority to emancipate her slaves. He made provision for them (see Sparks, *Life of Washington*, 545). In addition to freeing William Lee, he also gave him an annuity of thirty dollars per year for the rest of his life, plus food and clothing (Sparks, *Life of Washington*, 546). G. W. P. Custis reported that Lee also was given a house and $150 per year (Custis, *Recollections and Private Memoirs*, 157).

124. Ellis, *His Excellency*, book on tape.

125. Richardson, *Messages and Papers of the Presidents*, 1:205–16.

126. Washington to the Philadelphia clergy, March 3, 1797, GWP, 35:416.
127. "Circular to the Governors of the States," June 8, 1783, ibid., 26:496.
128. Washington to Col. Lewis Nicola, May 22, 1782, ibid., 24:272–73.
129. See GWP, 24:273, note.
130. GWP, 35:229; Schroeder, *Maxims of George Washington* (1989), 139.
131. This material is taken from McDowell, *In God We Trust*, 63–69, and is used by permission.
132. Washington to John Banister, April 21, 1778, GWP, 11:291.
133. GWP, 10:195.
134. Quoted in Brown, "Centennial Oration of Valley Forge," 61.
135. Quoted in McDowell, *Revolutionary War*, 128.
136. Wilbur, *Making of Washington*, 196.
137. Brown, "Centennial Oration of Valley Forge," 61.
138. Wilbur, *Making of Washington*, 195.
139. GWP, 11:291–92.
140. McDowell, *The Revolutionary War*, 131
141. Bancroft, *History of the United States*, 6:41.
142. Washington to the president of Congress, December 23, 1777, GWP, 10:196.
143. Brown, "Centennial Oration of Valley Forge," 66.
144. Ibid., 68.
145. Johnson, *Washington*, 120–21.
146. M'Guire, *Religious Opinions and Character of Washington*, 159.
147. Custis, *Recollections and Private Memoirs*, 275; see also M'Guire, *Religious Opinions and Character of Washington*, 159, and Johnson, *Washington*, 104.
148. Lancaster, *American Revolution*, 42.
149. GWP, 11:354. For a description of the thanksgiving at Valley Forge, see Sparks, *Life of Washington*, 267.

150. Washington to the Reverend Samuel Langdon on September 28, 1789, GWP, 30:416.

151. Henry Lee, "Oration on the Death of General Washington, Pronounced Before Both Houses of Congress, on December 16, 1799," in Custis, *Recollections and Private Memoirs*, 622, 618–19.

152. *An American Dictionary of the English Language* (1828), s.v. "Providence."

153. Washington to Joseph Reed, October 18, 1780, GWP 20:213.

154. GWP, 1:66.

155. Ibid., 1:70.

156. Washington to Robert Dinwiddie, ibid., 1:76.

157. Ibid., 3:294.

158. Ibid., 3:301. This and the previous letter are two of possibly only three letters that remain of Washington's correspondence with his wife; she burned all of his letters to her after his death.

159. Draper, *King's Mountain and Its Heroes*, 52–53.

160. Ibid.

161. Custis, *Recollections and Private Memoirs*, 305.

162. Ibid., 411.

163. George Washington Bicentennial Commission, *History of the Bicentennial Celebration, Literature Series*, 52.

164. Ibid.

165. Beliles and McDowell, *America's Providential History*, 161.

166. Irving, *Life of Washington*, 2:310–17.

167. Ibid., 2:317.

168. Sparks, *Life of Washington*, 197; Kirkland, *Memoirs of Washington*, 296.

169. See Beliles and McDowell, *America's Providential History*, 161–67.

170. Washington to Henry Knox, February 20, 1784, GWP, 27:340–41.

171. Kirkland, *Memoirs of Washington*, 355.

172. Washington to Bryan Fairfax, March 1, 1778, GWP, 11:3.

173. GWP, 27:1.
174. Ibid., 12:365.
175. Cited in Custis, *Recollections and Private Memoirs*, 214.
176. Washington to the president of Congress, December 20, 1776, GWP, 6:402.
177. Ibid., 6:462, note.
178. Resolve of Congress, December 27, 1776, ibid., 6:460.
179. Sparks, *Life of Washington*, 209; Kirkland, *Memoirs of Washington*, 313.
180. Washington to Robert Morris, George Clymer, and George Walton, January 1, 1777, GWP, 6:464.
181. Quoted in Custis, *Recollections and Private Memoirs*, 218. Lee acted out of either fear, incompetence, a means to undermine Washington, or treason. Custis offered evidence for the latter; see *Recollections and Private Memoirs*, 292.
182. Sparks, *Life of Washington*, 492.
183. Ibid., 544.
184. Kirkland, *Memoirs of Washington*, 79; Headley, *Washington*, 23.
185. See Sparks, *Life of Washington*, 93; Lossing, *Mount Vernon and Its Associations*, 86.
186. GWP, 11:291–92.
187. Richardson, *Messages and Papers of the Presidents*, 1:205–16.
188. Ibid.
189. It is clear from the context of Washington's writings that he refers to Christianity when he uses the term *religion*; for example, he writes, "the blessed Religion revealed in the word of God" (from "Fragments of the Discarded First Inaugural Address," in Allen, *Washington*, 454).
190. For more on this, see McDowell, *America, a Christian Nation*.
191. GWP, 30:453.
192. Washington to the Philadelphia clergy, March 3, 1797, ibid., 35:416.
193. Custis, *Recollections and Private Memoirs*, 513.

194. GWP, 3:479–80.

195. General orders, July 5, 1775, ibid., 3:312.

196. Sparks, *Life of Washington*, 143.

197. GWP, 30:416.

198. See Lossing, *Mount Vernon and Its Associations*, 237.

199. Ibid., 245–46.

200. GWP, 30:321.

201. Ibid., 3:492.

202. General orders, November 5, 1775, GWP, 4:65.

203. Ibid., 30:416.

204. Custis, *Recollections and Private Memoirs*, 97.

205. Washington to John McDowell, September 2, 1798, GWP, 36:421.

206. Washington to George Mason, April 5, 1769, ibid., 2:501.

207. Ibid., 33:166.

208. Ibid., 3:431.

209. Quoted in Custis, *Recollections and Private Memoirs*, 214.

210. Washington to Robert Dinwiddie, May 29, 1754, GWP, 1:60.

211. See Sparks, *Life of Washington*, 105.

212. Kirkland, *Memoirs of Washington*, 291.

213. Custis, *Recollections and Private Memoirs*, 192.

214. Kirkland, *Memoirs of Washington*, 320–21; Custis, *Recollections and Private Memoirs*, 191–92.

215. Custis, *Recollections and Private Memoirs*, 202.

216. Ibid., 217–21; Kirkland, *Memoirs of Washington*, 320–31, 345.

217. Kirkland, *Memoirs of Washington*, 345; Custis, *Recollections and Private Memoirs*, 220–21.

218. Kirkland, *Memoirs of Washington*, 346; Custis, *Recollections and Private Memoirs*, 223–24.

219. Custis, *Recollections and Private Memoirs*, 242.

220. George Washington Bicentennial Commission, *History of the Bicentennial Celebration, Literature Series*, 35.

221. Washington, *Address to the United Baptist Churches*, 3.

222. GWP, 1:67.

223. Flexner, *Washington in the Revolution*, 507.

224. Ibid.

225. Kirkland, *Memoirs of Washington*, 402.

226. Sparks, *Life of Washington*, 406.

227. Ibid.

228. GWP, 30:288.

229. Custis, *Recollections and Private Memoirs*, 109.

230. See Washington to Col. John Stanwix, March 4, 1758, GWP, 2:166.

231. GWP, 11:237.

232. Sparks, *Life of Washington*, 375–76.

233. Kirkland, *Memoirs of Washington*, 370.

234. Ibid., 387–88.

235. Washington to Lund Washington, May 19, 1780, GWP, 18:293.

236. Kirkland, *Memoirs of Washington*, 143.

237. Washington to Arthur Young, December 12, 1793, GWP, 33:175–76.

238. Custis, *Recollections and Private Memoirs*, 41.

239. See GWP, 2:242, note 41.

240. Ibid., 2:242.

241. Washington to Martha Washington, June 18, 1775, ibid., 3:293–94.

242. Washington to Martha Washington, June 23, 1775, ibid., 3:300–301.

243. Washington to John Augustine Washington, June 20, 1775, ibid., 3:300.

244. Kirkland, *Memoirs of Washington*, 265.

245. Washington to Eleanor Parke Custis, January 16, 1795, GWP, 34:91–92.

246. GWP, 35:294–96.

247. Washington to George Washington Parke Custis, June 4, 1797, ibid., 35:458–59.

248. Custis, *Recollections and Private Memoirs*, 88.

249. GWP, 30:399.

250. Custis, *Recollections and Private Memoirs*, 145–46.

251. GWP, 30:399.

252. Home of Mary Washington, Fredericksburg, Virginia, "Facsimile of the Will of Mary Washington, as Registered in the Clerk's Office at Fredericksburg, Virginia."

253. Custis, *Recollections and Private Memoirs*, 235.

254. Lossing, *Mount Vernon and Its Associations*, 287.

255. Sparks, *Life of Washington*, 473; Lossing, *Mount Vernon and Its Associations*, 285.

256. Sparks, *Life of Washington*, 76–77.

257. Custis, *Recollections and Private Memoirs*, 89.

258. Ibid., 527.

259. Ibid.

260. Ibid.

261. Kirkland, *Memoirs of Washington*, 153.

262. Ibid., 235.

263. Ibid., 59.

264. Kirkland, *Memoirs of Washington*, 153.

265. George Washington Bicentennial Commission, *History of the Bicentennial Celebration, Literature Series*, 31.

266. Ibid., 32.

267. Sparks, *Life of Washington*, 490.

268. Jones, *Ashbel Green*, 265.

269. Custis, *Recollections and Private Memoirs*, 430–31.

270. Ibid., 315.

271. Irving, *Life of Washington*, 7:66–68.

272. From the diary of a soldier published by Irving Bacheller, in an address by E. M. Bruce, February 26, 1932, delivered in Germany on the bicentennial celebration of Washington's birth in George Washington Bicentennial Commission, *History of the Bicentennial Celebration, Foreign Participation*, 147.

273. George Washington Bicentennial Commission, *History of the Bicentennial Celebration, Foreign Participation*, 462.
274. Johnson, *Washington*, 209.
275. Kirkland, *Memoirs of Washington*, 50.
276. Custis, *Recollections and Private Memoirs*, 163.
277. Ibid., 429.
278. Kirkland, *Memoirs of Washington*, 162.
279. GWP, 1:325.
280. Washington to the president of Congress, December 23, 1777, ibid., 10:196.
281. Kirkland, *Memoirs of Washington*, 415–17.
282. See Washington, *Diaries*, 30–117, 82.
283. Wirt, *Patrick Henry*, 45; see also Sparks, *Life of Washington*, 100; Custis, *Recollections and Private Memoirs*, 153; Lossing, *Mount Vernon and Its Associations*, 92.
284. Custis, *Recollections and Private Memoirs*, 136, from Charles Francis Adams, *The Life and Works of John Adams*, 10 vols. (1850–56, reprint, Washington DC : Ross and Perry, 2002), 2:415–18.
285. Smith, *Adams*, 1:200–201.
286. Custis, *Recollections and Private Memoirs*, 136; Kirkland, *Memoirs of Washington*, 223–24.
287. Adams, *Book of Abigail and John*, 89.
288. GWP, 3:292–93.
289. Ibid., 3:293–94.
290. Ibid., 3:295.
291. Ibid., 3:296–98.
292. Ibid., 3:299.
293. Kirkland, *Memoirs of Washington*, 235.
294. Custis, *Recollections and Private Memoirs*, 401.
295. Kirkland, *Memoirs of Washington*, 402.
296. Sparks, *Life of Washington*, 218.
297. Johnson, *Washington*, 244.

298. Sparks, *Life of Washington*, 492.

299. Johnson, *Washington*, 247.

300. Washington to Alexander Hamilton, August 28, 1788, GWP, 30:67.

301. Weems, *History of Washington*, 24–25.

302. Custis, *Recollections and Private Memoirs*, 132–34.

303. Washington to Henry Laurens, January 31, 1778, GWP, 10:410–11.

304. Sparks, *Life of Washington*, 254.

305. Ibid., 252.

306. Washington to G. W. P. Custis, November 15, 1796, GWP, 35:283.

307. Washington to Lund Washington, November 26, 1775, ibid., 4:115.

308. M'Guire, *Religious Opinions and Character of Washington*, 190.

309. Ibid.

310. Ibid., 194; Sparks, *Life of Washington*, 385.

311. See Sparks, *Life of Washington*, 384, 549.

312. See ibid., 385; M'Guire, *Religious Opinions and Character of Washington*, 188.

313. Sparks, *Life of Washington*, 385–86.

314. Custis, *Recollections and Private Memoirs*, 156.

315. Ibid., 421–22.

316. Washington to the Reverend John Lathrop, June 22, 1788, GWP 30:5.

317. Irving, *Washington*, 7:69.

318. Custis, *Recollections and Private Memoirs*, 214.

319. Sparks, *Life of Washington*, 106.

320. Ibid., 258.

321. Sparks, *Life of Washington*, 120–21; see also GWP, 3:245–46.

322. Custis, *Recollections and Private Memoirs*, 155.

323. Ibid., 156.

324. See Kirkland, *Memoirs of Washington*, 278; Washington to British Gen. Thomas Gage, August 20, 1775, GWP, 3:431.

325. Kirkland, *Memoirs of Washington*, 370.

326. Ibid., 371.

327. Custis, *Recollections and Private Memoirs*, 366.

328. Ibid., 389.

329. Sparks, *Life of Washington*, 256.

330. Kirkland, *Memoirs of Washington*, 347.

331. GWP, 16:116–17.

332. Sparks, *Life of Washington*, 152.

333. Jones, *Ashbel Green*, 267.

334. George Washington Bicentennial Commission, *History of the Bicentennial Celebration, Literature Series*, 54.

335. M'Guire, *Religious Opinions and Character of Washington*, 194.

336. GWP, 3:309.

337. Ibid., 5:245.

338. General orders for May 2, 1778, ibid., 11:343.

PART 3: THE LEGACY OF GEORGE WASHINGTON

1. Custis, *Recollections and Private Memoirs*, 215; see also, George Washington Bicentennial Commission, *History of the Bicentennial Celebration, Foreign Participation*, 403, and Osborn, *Washington Speaks for Himself*, x.

2. Custis, *Recollections and Private Memoirs*, 215.

3. For example, see Bancroft, *Eulogy on Washington*, and Holmes, *A Nation Mourns*. Various books of compilations of orations and sermons have been published; see, for example: *Memory of Washington*, *Eulogies and Orations*, and *Selection of Orations and Eulogies*.

4. Payson, *Sermon*.

5. Morse, *Prayer and Sermon*, 28.

6. Custis, *Recollections and Private Memoirs*, 322.

7. Sparks, *Life of Washington*, 455.

8. Ibid., 456.
9. Osborn, *Washington Speaks for Himself,* xi.
10. Ibid., iv.
11. Dr. John Coakley Letsom to a friend in Boston, in M'Guire, *Religious Opinions and Character of Washington,* 326.
12. "Circular to the Governors of the States," June 8, 1783, GWP, 26:496.
13. Henry Lee, "Oration on the Death of General Washington," in Custis, *Recollections and Private Memoirs,* 622, 618–19.
14. Washington to Lucretia Wilhemina Van Winter, March 30, 1785, GWP, 28:120.
15. Jones, *Ashbel Green,* 265.
16. Sparks, *Life of Washington,* 493.

Bibliography

Adams, Abigail. *The Book of Abigail and John: Selected Letters of the Adams Family, 1762–1784.* Edited by L. H. Butterfield, Marc Friedlaender, and Mary-Jo Kline. Cambridge, MA: Harvard University Press, 1975.

Adams, Samuel. *The Rights of the Colonists.* Old South Leaflets, no. 173. Boston: Old South Meeting-house, n.d.

Allen, W. B., comp. and ed. *George Washington: A Collection.* Indianapolis: Liberty Fund, 1988.

Ames, Fisher. *Works of Fisher Ames.* Edited by W. B. Allen. 2 vols. 1854. Reprint, Indianapolis: Liberty Classics, 1983.

Andrews, Marietta Minnigerode. *George Washington's Country.* New York: Dutton, 1930.

Bancroft, Aaron. *An Eulogy on the Character of the Late Gen. George Washington.* Worcester: Isaiah Thomas, 1800.

Bancroft, George. *History of the United States.* 6 vols. Boston: Little, Brown, 1878.

Barton, David. *The Question of Freemasonry and the Founding Fathers.* Aledo, TX: Wallbuilders, 2005.

Beliles, Mark, and Doug Anderson. *Contending for the Constitution.* Charlottesville, VA: Providence Foundation, 2005.

———, and Stephen K. McDowell. *America's Providential History.* Charlottesville, VA: Providence Foundation, 1989.

Boller, Paul F. *George Washington and Religion.* Dallas: Southern Methodist University Press, 1963.

Brown, Henry Armit. "Centennial Oration of Valley Forge." In *The Christian History of the American Revolution: Consider and Ponder.* Compiled by Verna Hall. San Francisco: Foundation for American Christian Education, 1976.

Custis, George Washington Parke. *Recollections and Private Memoirs of the Life and Character of Washington by George Washington Parke Custis, with Memoir of George Washington Parke Custis by His Daughter: With the Epistolary Correspondence Between Washington and Custis.* Edited by Benson J. Lossing. Philadelphia: Englewood, 1859.

Davies, Samuel. *Religion and Patriotism: The Constituents of a Good Soldier, A Sermon Preached to Captain Overton's Independent Company of Volunteers, Raised in Hanover County, Virginia, August 17, 1755.* Philadelphia: Buckland, Wars, and Field, 1756.

Draper, Lyman C. *King's Mountain and Its Heroes: History of the Battle of King's Mountain, October 7th, 1780, and the Events Which Led to It.* 1881. Reprint, Baltimore: Genealogical Publishing Co., 1983.

Ellis, Joseph. *His Excellency: George Washington.* New York, Knopf, 2004.

Eulogies and Orations on the Life and Death of General George Washington. Boston: Manning and Loring, 1800.

Everett, Edward. *The Life of George Washington.* New York: Sheldon, 1860.

Farrand, Max. *The Records of the Federal Convention of 1787.* 3 vols. New Haven: Yale University Press, 1911.

Fiske, John. *The Critical Period of American History, 1783–1789.* New York: Houghton, Mifflin, 1902.

Fitzpatrick, John C., ed. *The Last Will and Testament of George Washington.* Washington DC: Mount Vernon Ladies' Association, 1939.

Flexner, James Thomas. *George Washington: The Forge of Experience (1732–1775).* Boston: Little, Brown, 1965.

———. *George Washington in the American Revolution, 1775–1783.* Boston: Little, Brown, 1967.

Force, Peter, comp. *American Archives.* 9 vols. 1837–53. Reprint, New York, Johnson Reprint, 1972.

Freeman, Douglas Southall. *George Washington: A Biography.* 7 vols. New York: Scribner, 1948–57.

George Washington Bicentennial Commission. *History of the George Washington Bicentennial Celebration, Foreign Participation.* Washington DC: George Washington Bicentennial Commission, 1932.

———. *History of the George Washington Bicentennial Celebration, Literature Series.* Washington DC: George Washington Bicentennial Commission, 1932.

Hall, Verna M., comp. *The Christian History of the American Revolution: Consider and Ponder.* San Francisco: Foundation for American Christian Education, 1976.

———, comp. *George Washington: The Character and Influence of One Man.* San Francisco: Foundation for American Christian Education, 1999.

Headley, J. T. *The Illustrated Life of Washington.* New York: Bill, 1859.

Henriques, Peter R. *America's First President: George Washington.* Fort Washington, PA: Eastern National, 2002.

Holmes, David L., ed. *A Nation Mourns: Bishop James Madison's Memorial Eulogy on the Death of George Washington, Delivered February 22, 1800 in Bruton Parish Church,*

Williamsburg, Virginia. Mount Vernon: Mount Vernon Ladies' Association, 1999.

Irving, Washington. *Life of George Washington.* Knickerbocker Edition. 8 vols. New York: Putnam, 1897.

Jefferson, Thomas. *The Writings of Thomas Jefferson.* Edited by Andrew A. Lipscomb and Albert Ellery Bergh. 20 vols. Washington DC: Thomas Jefferson Memorial Association, 1903–4.

Johnson, William J. *George Washington, the Christian.* 1919. Reprint, Milford, MI: Mott Media, 1976.

Johnston, Elizabeth Bryant. *George Washington Day by Day.* Washington DC: n.p., 1894.

Jones, Joseph H. *The Life of Ashbel Green.* New York: Carter, 1849.

Kent, Donald H., ed. *Contrecoeur's Copy of George Washington's Journal for 1754.* Fort Washington, PA: Eastern National Park & Monument Association, 1989.

Kirkland, Caroline M. *Memoirs of Washington.* New York: Appleton, 1857.

Lancaster, Bruce. *The American Revolution.* Garden City, NY: Garden City Books, 1957.

Lecky, Robert, Jr. "The Proceedings of the Virginia Convention in the Town of Richmond on the 23rd of March, 1775." 1927. Reprint. Richmond: Saint John's Church, 1938.

Littell, John Stockton. *Washington—Christian.* Keene, NH: Hampshire Art Press, 1913.

Lossing, Benson J. *Mount Vernon and Its Associations.* New York: Townsend, 1859.

Love, W. DeLoss. *The Fast and Thanksgiving Days of New England.* Boston: Houghton, Mifflin, 1895.

McCullough, David. *1776.* New York: Simon & Schuster, 2005.

McDowell, Bart. *The Revolutionary War.* Washington DC: National Geographic Society, 1970.

McDowell, Stephen K. *America, a Christian Nation? Examining the Evidence of the Christian Foundation of America.* Charlottesville, VA: Providence Foundation, 2004.

———. *Building Godly Nations.* Charlottesville, VA: Providence Foundation, 2004.

———. *In God We Trust Tour Guide.* Charlottesville, VA: Providence Foundation, 1998.

Madison, James. *Notes of Debates in the Federal Convention of 1787.* New York: Norton, 1987.

Manship, James Renwick. "George Washington: Deist? Freemason? Christian?" *Providential Perspective* 15, no. 1 (February 2000): 1–8.

M'Clure, David. *A Discourse: Commemorative of the Death of General George Washington.* East-Windsor, CT: Pratt, 1800.

Meade, William. *Old Churches, Ministers and Families of Virginia.* 2 vols. Philadelphia: Lippincott, 1857.

Memory of Washington: Comprising a Sketch of His Life and Character . . . a Collection of Eulogies and Orations. Newport, RI: Farnsworth, 1800.

M'Guire, E. C. *The Religious Opinions and Character of Washington.* New York: Harper & Brothers, 1836.

Moore, Charles. *The Family Life of George Washington.* New York: Houghton Mifflin, 1926.

Morris, B. F. *Christian Life and Character of the Civil Institutions of the United States.* Philadelphia: Childs, 1864.

Morse, Jedidiah. *A Prayer and Sermon, Delivered at Charlestown, December 31, 1799, on the Death of George Washington . . . with an Additional Sketch of His Life.* London: Bateson, 1800.

Muhlenberg, Henry Melchoir. *The Journals of Henry Melchoir Muhlenberg.* Translated by Theodore Tappert and John Dobestein. 3 vols. Philadelphia: Evangelical Lutheran Ministerium of Pennsylvania and Adjacent States, 1942–58.

Novak, Michael, and Jana Novak. *Washington's God: Religion, Liberty, and the Father of Our Country.* New York: Basic Books, 2006.

Osborn, Lucretia Perry. *Washington Speaks for Himself.* New York: Scribner, 1927.

Paulding, James K. *A Life of Washington.* 2 vols. New York: Harper & Brothers, 1835.

Payson, Phillips. *A Sermon Delivered at Chelsea, January 14, 1800: A Day Devoted by the Inhabitants of Said Town, to Pay Their Tribute of Grief on the Sorrowful Event of the Death of General Washington.* Charlestown, MA: Etheridge, 1800.

Pickman, Benjamin, Jr. *An Oration Pronounced February 22, 1797, Before the Inhabitants of the Town of Salem, in Massachusetts, Assembled to Commemorate the Birthday of George Washington.* Salem: Cushing, 1797.

Richardson, James D. *A Compilation of the Messages and Papers of the Presidents.* 10 vols. Washington DC: Government Printing Office, 1896–99.

Rush, Richard. *Washington in Domestic Life, from Original Letters and Manuscripts.* Philadelphia: Lippincott, 1857.

Schroeder, John Frederick. *Life and Times of Washington.* 2 vols. New York: Johnson, Fry, 1857.

———, comp. *Maxims of George Washington: Political, Military, Social, Moral, and Religious.* New York: Appleton, 1854.

———, comp. *Maxims of George Washington: Political, Military, Social, Moral, and Religious.* Mount Vernon, VA: Mount Vernon Ladies' Association, 1989.

A Selection of Orations and Eulogies, Pronounced in Different Parts of the United States, in Commemoration of the Life, Virtues, and Pre-eminent Services of Gen. George Washington. Amherst, MA: Preston, 1800.

Slaughter, Philip. *Christianity the Key to the Character and Career of Washington.* New York: Whittaker, 1886.

Smith, Page. *John Adams.* Garden City, NY: Doubleday, 1962.

Sparks, Jared. *The Life of George Washington.* Boston: Little, Brown, 1860.

Washington, George. *Address to the United Baptist Churches, May, 1789.* Old South Leaflets, no. 65. Boston: Old South Association, n.d.

———. *The Diaries of George Washington.* Edited by Donald Jackson and Dorothy Twohig. 6 vols. Charlottesville: University Press of Virginia, 1976–79.

———. *The Writings of George Washington from the Original Manuscript Sources, 1745–1799.* Edited by John C. Fitzpatrick. 39 volumes. Washington DC: U.S. Government Printing Office, 1931.

———. *Washington's Addresses to the Churches.* Old South Leaflets, no. 65. Boston: Old South Association, n.d.

———. *Writings of George Washington.* Edited by Jared Sparks. 12 vols. Boston: Russell, Shattuck, and Williams, 1836.

Watson, Henry B. *George Washington, Architect of the Constitution.* Daytona Beach, FL: Patriotic Education, 1983.

Weems, Mason Locke. *A History of the Life and Death, Virtues and Exploits of General George Washington.* 1800. Reprint, New York: Macy-Massius, 1927.

———. *Mason Locke Weems: His Works and Ways.* Edited by Emily Ellsworth Ford Skeel. 3 vols. New York, 1929.

Wilbur, William. *The Making of George Washington.* DeLand, FL: Patriotic Education, 1973.

Willard, Joseph. *An Address in Latin, by Joseph Willard . . . and a Discourse in English, by David Tappan . . . Delivered Before the University in Cambridge, Feb. 21, 1800, in Solemn Commemoration of Gen. George Washington.* Charlestown, MA: Etheridge, 1800.

Wirt, William. *Sketches of the Life and Character of Patrick Henry.* Philadelphia: Webster, 1818.

Wylie, Theodore William John. *Washington a Christian: A Discourse Preached February 23, 1862, in the First Reformed Presbyterian Church, Philadelphia, by the Pastor.* Philadelphia: Martien, 1862.

INDEX

STEPHEN McDOWELL is the cofounder and president of the Providence Foundation, a nonprofit Christian educational organizational. He is the author or coauthor of numerous books and articles, a the critically acclaimed *America's Providential History*. He lives in Charlottesville, Virginia, with his family.

DAVID VAUGHAN is the pastor of Liberty Christian Church, director of Liberty Leadership Institute, and president of Liberty Classical School. Vaughan lives in O'Fallon, Missouri.

Jacket design: Gore Studio, Inc.
Cover Image: Library of Congress

Printed in the USA
CPSIA information can be obtained
at www.ICGtesting.com
JSHW012019140824
68134JS00033B/2779

9 781684 423491